AI for Absolute Beginners

A Non-Technical Guide to Understanding Artificial Intelligence

---

Akash Sunil Shahade

Senior Engineer, AI/ML

First Edition, 2026

Made with ♥ on the Notion Press Platform
www.notionpress.com

To my family,

who gave me the foundation to ask questions.

And to you, the curious reader, holding this book.

You picked it up. That already says something.

Contents

Preface

Why this book exists and who it is for

There is a version of this book that opens with statistics. Global AI market size. Number of AI startups funded last year. Percentage of jobs projected to be automated by some future date. Charts with steep upward curves.

This is not that version.

I am a Senior Engineer who builds and deploys AI and ML applications professionally. I spend my working days inside the kinds of systems this book describes. And even I find the noise around AI exhausting sometimes. The people who want you to be excited are usually selling something: a product, a course, a stock, an idea of themselves as visionaries. The people who want you to be frightened are also usually selling something: a newsletter, a political position, and a sense of urgency that keeps you reading.

This book has a different goal. It wants to make you independent of both camps.

Not because AI does not matter. It matters enormously. It is already reshaping medicine, education, finance, creative work, and the way information reaches you every single day. But the way to engage with something that matters is with clear eyes, not with panic or euphoria.

I grew up in a household where nobody explained technology. Computers arrived, then the internet, then smartphones, and each time the message from the world seemed to figure it out yourself or get left behind. I did not want to write another book for people who had already figured it out. I wanted to write the book I wish had existed when I was trying to understand things that felt designed to confuse me.

So, this book does not assume you know anything about AI, computers, or technology. It does not require you to be young, technical, or already curious about this topic. It requires only that you are willing to sit with an idea long enough to actually understand it.

Who This Book Is For

This book is for the professional who needs to understand AI well enough to have an informed opinion in meetings. For the parents who want to understand what their children are growing up with. For the retiree who keeps hearing about AI on the news and wants to know what it actually is. For the student who is about to enter a workforce that will be shaped by these technologies. For anyone who has ever typed something into ChatGPT and wondered what was actually happening on the other side of that conversation.

If any of those descriptions fit you, this book was written for you.

What This Book Is Not

This is not a technical manual. You will not learn to build an AI system or write code.

This is not a prediction book. You will not find firm claims about exactly how many jobs AI will eliminate by a specific year, because anyone making those claims with certainty is guessing.

This is not a hype book or a fear book. Both genres are well stocked. The world does not need another one either.

What you will find here is a clear, honest, and clear explanation of what AI is, how it works in plain terms, where it is already present in your daily life, what it can and cannot do, what the real risks are, and how to think about all of it in a way that serves you for years to come.

How to Use This Book

Read it for the first time. Each chapter builds on the previous one and the arc matters. Each chapter ends with a short summary of the key ideas. These are not shortcuts; they are anchors. After you finish the book, you can return to any summary to refresh your thinking quickly.

A Note on Speed

AI is changing faster than any book can track. By the time you read this, new tools will have been released, and some specific examples may feel dated. That is inevitable and fine.

The fundamentals do not change at the same speed. Understanding what AI is, how it learns, and where it goes wrong: these are durable ideas. I am giving you the framework, not just the current facts. The framework will serve you long after the specific tools it describes have been replaced by the next generation.

Let's begin.

CHAPTER ONE

What AI Really Is

No buzzwords. No hype. Just the truth.

Here is the sentence this entire book rests on: AI finds patterns in large amounts of data and uses those patterns to make predictions.

That is, it. Everything else, the chatbots, the image generators, the hiring algorithms, the self-driving cars, the cancer-detecting medical scanners, all of it is a variation on that one idea applied to different types of data at different scales of sophistication. When people tell you AI is magic, or that it thinks like a human, or that it is about to become conscious, they are describing something that feels true from the outside but is not accurate on the inside.

So let us see it clearly.

The Pattern Recognition Machine

Your phone keyboard suggests the next word as you type. It has seen how you write before, and how millions of other people write, and it has learned: after these particular words in this context, these are the words most likely to come next.

It is not thinking. It is pattern-matching at an extraordinary speed.

A streaming service puts a show at the top of your homepage because it noticed that people who watched the same three shows you watched last month also watched a fourth show, and most of them kept watching past the first ten minutes. Pattern found, recommendation made. It does not know you as a person. It knows your pattern.

A radiologist uses an AI tool to review a chest scan. The AI highlights a small shadow that a tired doctor might overlook at the end of a long shift. It does this because it was trained on hundreds of thousands of scans labelled by expert radiologists over many years. Pattern recognition applied to medical images.

Story: Four Hundred Million People, One AI System

In January and February 2025, Prayagraj hosted the Maha Kumbh Mela. Roughly four hundred to six hundred million people attended the course of the event, making it the largest human gathering ever recorded. To put that number in perspective, it is larger than the entire population of the United States and Brazil combined, all in one place over a few weeks.

Managing crowd safety at that scale is simply beyond what any human team can track in real time. There are too many people, too many entry points, too many things happening at once.

The Uttar Pradesh government deployed an AI-powered system across the Mela grounds. Hundreds of cameras monitored crowd density continuously, feeding data into a system that tracked the flow of people across different zones. When density in an area crossed a threshold that previous data had identified as dangerous, the system flagged it automatically. Security personnel on the ground could be redirected before a situation became critical rather than after.

The system also helped reunite separated families. Lost persons, including elderly pilgrims and young children who had become separated from their groups, were identified faster through facial recognition tools than through manual search processes that had been used in previous years. Families were reunited in minutes in cases that might previously have taken hours.

The AI did not understand what Kumbh Mela means to the people who travel from across India and the world to attend it. It had no idea of the spiritual weight of the occasion, or what it means for a family to make that journey together. It simply watched patterns of movement across thousands of camera feeds, measured density against historical data, and sent alerts when the numbers suggested risk.

Pattern recognition applied to the right problem at the right scale. That is what made the difference.

The same underlying principle, running at vastly different scales and applied to vastly different problems. This is what AI is.

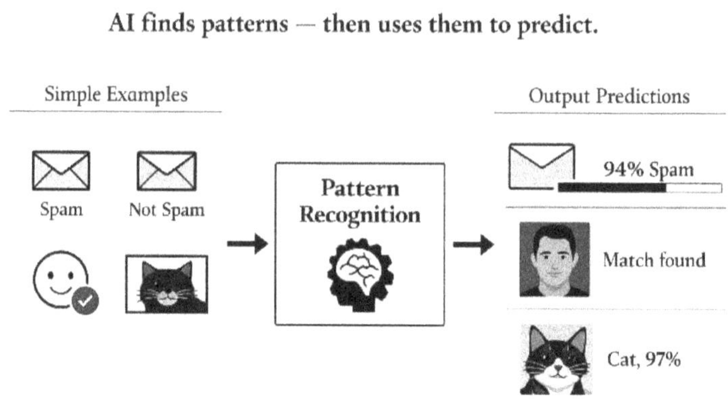

Figure 1.1: Pattern Recognition: From Simple Examples to Complex Predictions

The Russian Dolls: AI, Machine Learning, and Deep Learning

You will hear these three terms used interchangeably, which frustrates anyone who understands them, because they are not the same thing. They are nested concepts, like Russian dolls, and the distinction matters.

AI is the outermost doll. The broadest possible term. It covers anything a computer does that resembles intelligent behavior. Your thermostat learning you like the temperature lower at night is AI. A chess program playing at grandmaster level is AI. The spam filter is an AI. The term was introduced in 1956 by computer scientist John McCarthy at a conference at Dartmouth College.

Machine Learning is the middle doll. These are systems that improve experience without being explicitly programmed for every situation. Traditional software is given explicit rules: if the email contains this word, mark it as spam. Machine learning software is given examples and finds the rules itself: here are ten thousand spam emails and ten thousand legitimate ones, figure out what distinguishes them. The spam filter that gets better over time is machine learning. Nobody programmed a rule about every new scam. The system learned it.

Deep Learning is the innermost doll. These are neural networks with many stacked layers, capable of finding patterns of extraordinary complexity in images, sound, and text. Deep learning powers modern language tools, enables facial recognition, and makes voice assistants possible. It is called deep because of those many layers, not because it understands anything deeply. Understanding, in the human sense, is not part of the picture at all.

All deep learning is machine learning. All machine learning is AI. But not all AI is machine learning, and not all machine learning is deep learning. When ChatGPT writes you a cover letter, that is all three simultaneously. When your thermostat adjusts to your schedule, that is AI but probably not deep learning.

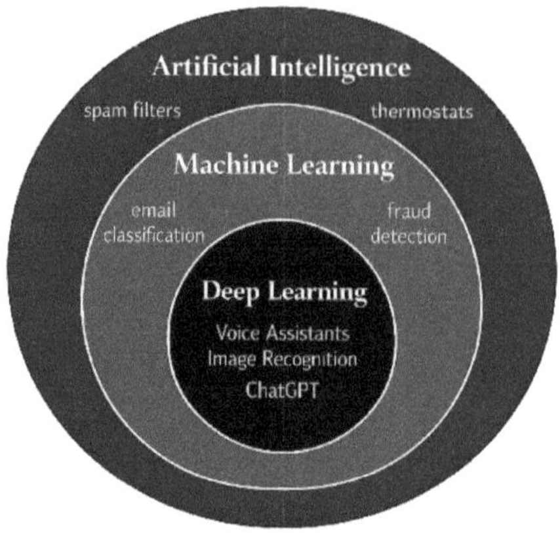

Deep Learning is a subset of Machine Learning, which is a subset of Artificial Intelligence.

Figure 1.2: AI, Machine Learning, Deep Learning: The Nested Relationship

A Short History Worth Knowing

AI did not arrive suddenly. The ideas behind it stretch back decades, and understanding a little of that history helps you see why it feels so sudden now even though it is not.

In the 1950s and 1960s, researchers were optimistic. They believed that if you could give a computer the right rules, it would reason like a human. These early systems worked reasonably well in narrow situations but collapsed when they encountered anything outside their rule set. The world was too messy for rules to cover it completely.

Progress slowed in what researchers later called AI winters; periods when funding dried up because the technology had not delivered on its promises. There were two major winters, roughly in the 1970s and again in the late 1980s.

What changed was not a single invention, but the meeting of three conditions that had been developing separately for decades.

The first was data. AI learns from examples. For most of its history, examples were scarce. Then the internet connected billions of people, and those people generated text, images, purchases, searches, and conversations on a scale that had never existed before. The raw material for training AI systems became available in quantities earlier researchers could not have imagined.

The second was computing power. Graphics processing units, originally designed for video game rendering, turned out to be extraordinarily well-suited for the mathematical operations that machine learning requires. Hardware that once required a room full of expensive equipment became accessible and affordable.

The third was better architecture. In 2017, a team of researchers at Google published a paper titled "Attention Is All You Need" describing a new approach called the transformer. This architecture proved far better than previous approaches at handling complex relationships in language. Almost every powerful language tool in use today is built on some variation of this 2017 insight.

Data, computing power, and architecture: all three converged at the same time. The result was AI systems capable enough to be useful in everyday life for the first time in technology history.

A Useful Mental Model

Think of AI as a very capable new employee who has read everything in the company library but has never actually worked in the office.

This person has a remarkable breadth of knowledge. They can draft, summarize, research, and explain at speeds and volumes no human can match. But they are unreliable in specific ways. They can be confidently wrong. They do not have common sense that comes from experience. They cannot tell the difference between something they know and something they have assembled from similar-sounding pieces of information they encountered while reading.

Working with AI effectively means using this employee's extraordinary capabilities while compensating for these specific limitations. Give them clear briefs. Check their work on anything important. Do not ask them to exercise judgment in areas where lived experience matters.

The more precisely you identify which tasks they are reliable at and which they are not, the more useful they become.

What AI Is Genuinely Good At

AI is extraordinary at recognizing patterns in images. Medical imaging AI can detect certain cancers from scans with accuracy matching experienced specialists, and it can do this without fatigue. Quality control systems in manufacturing use AI to catch product defects at speeds human inspectors cannot match.

AI is excellent at processing and generating languages. Summarizing long documents, translating between languages, answering questions on topics well covered in its training, drafting text: these are things current language tools do well enough to be useful in daily work.

AI is outstanding at prediction problems where there is abundant historical data. Fraud detection, demand forecasting, recommendation systems: anywhere there is a large dataset with clear past outcomes to learn from, AI can find patterns that human analysts would miss.

AI also handles games and defined-rule environments at a level that leaves human capability behind entirely. Chess, the strategy game Go, and most video games with fixed rules have all been mastered by AI systems.

What AI Handles Poorly

AI has very little common sense. It has no internal model of how the physical world works, how causation operates, or what is obvious to any human adult. You know that if you put a glass on the edge of a table and it falls, it will not fall upward. AI has no equivalent to this understanding.

AI does not know when it is wrong. This is perhaps the most practically important limitation. A human expert who has reached the edge of their knowledge will usually signal uncertainty. Many AI systems will give you a confident-sounding answer even when that answer is fabricated. The term for this is hallucination: the system generates something that sounds plausible and fluent but is simply not true.

AI struggles with novel situations. When a situation has no close equivalent in training data, the system is essentially guessing analogy. Sometimes the analogy is close enough. Sometimes it is wrong in ways that are not obvious.

AI cannot reason for ethics the way humans do. It can produce text about ethical principles, but it does not have values, feelings, or the lived experience that shapes moral judgment.

AI Excels At	AI Struggles With
Image Recognition	Common Sense
Language Processing	Knowing When It is Wrong
Prediction from Data	Novel Situations
Game-Playing	Ethical Judgment
Spotting Patterns at Scale	Emotional Understanding

Figure 1.3: What AI Does Well vs Where It Struggles

The Intelligence Myth

The phrase "artificial intelligence" is doing a lot of misleading work. When most people hear the word intelligence, they think of awareness, curiosity, creativity, and the ability to navigate unexpected situations with good judgment. When AI researchers use it, they mean something far more specific: the ability to perform tasks that would require intelligence if a human were doing them.

Consider a calculator. It computes large calculations faster and more accurately than any human. Nobody calls a calculator intelligent, because it simply follows fixed rules at high speed. It does not understand what the numbers mean.

AI is, in a meaningful sense, a vastly more powerful and flexible calculator. Instead of arithmetic rules, it has learned statistical patterns from data. Instead of computing numbers, it works with images, words, and sounds. But the fundamental nature of what it is doing is not so different: finding statistical regularities and applying them at extraordinary speed. There is no awareness behind it, no experience of what it is doing.

Knowing this helps you use AI well. Lean on its pattern-matching strengths: speed, scale, consistency. Compensate for its weaknesses: common sense, judgment, accountability. Stay in the relationship as the person who understands the actual situation.

Why This Matters to You

AI is already making decisions that affect your daily life whether you are aware of it or not.

The algorithm deciding whether your job application reaches a human recruiter is making a judgment call based on patterns it has learned. The system determining whether your loan application gets a human review is doing the same. The recommendations you see on shopping sites, news feeds, and entertainment platforms are all AI systems learning your patterns and presenting content calculated to keep you engaged.

Understanding AI does not protect you from all of this. But it changes your relationship to it entirely. You ask different questions. You notice things you would not have noticed before. You make more informed choices about which systems you trust, which you question, and which you push back against.

That is what this book is for.

The World Before AI Could Do This

To appreciate what AI actually does today, it helps to remember what was not possible even fifteen years ago.

In 2005, if you wanted to translate a paragraph from one language to another, you needed either a human translator or a basic rule-based translation program that produced results good enough to understand the gist but too awkward to use directly. Today, AI translation is good enough that professional translators frequently use it as a starting draft and refine it. That is a fundamentally different way of working.

In 2005, if you had a large set of customer feedback comments and wanted to understand the main themes, you needed a person to read them. Today, AI can summarize thousands of comments in seconds with reasonable accuracy.

In 2005, if a doctor wanted to know whether a scan showed early signs of a specific condition, they needed a specialist to look at it. Today, AI systems can provide a first-pass assessment that helps prioritize which scans need urgent attention.

None of this happened because someone invented something radically new in a single dramatic moment. It happened because decades of research, increasing availability of data, and dramatic improvements in computing hardware all converged. The speed of that convergence is what makes AI feel sudden, even though the underlying ideas are old.

How AI Sees the World Differently from You

One of the more disorienting things about AI, for people thinking about it carefully for the first time, is that it processes information in a way that is radically unlike human perception.

You see a photograph of a dog, and you immediately know it is a dog. You do not consciously process the pixels. You do not list features and compare them to a mental checklist. The recognition is instantaneous and feels effortless because it runs on a cognitive system shaped by a lifetime of experience with the world.

An AI image recognition system processes that same photograph as a grid of numerical values. Red channel: 247. Green channel: 203. Blue Channel 142. It passes these values through layers of mathematical transformations, each layer building a more abstract representation of the patterns in the image, until the final layer produces a probability distribution over possible labels: Dog at 94 percent probability. Cat at 3 percent. Fox at 2 percent.

The system arrives at the right answer. But the way it arrives there is nothing like the way you arrive there. There is no moment of recognition, no feeling of familiarity, no visual memory of dogs you have known.

This matters because it means AI systems can make errors that no human ever would and can be robust in ways that no human ever is. A human who has seen ten thousand dogs will struggle to identify a breed they have never encountered. An AI system trained on broad enough data can generalize across breeds it has never seen. But the same human who has seen ten thousand dogs will immediately recognize a dog when it is partly obscured, shown from an unusual angle, or wearing a costume. An AI system may fail in exactly those conditions.

Neither way of seeing is better in all circumstances. They are different and understanding that difference helps you predict where AI will be reliable and where it will not.

The Question of What AI Actually Understands

People sometimes argue about whether AI truly understands anything or is just sophisticated pattern matching. This can feel abstract, but it has practical implications.

Consider what happens when you ask an AI language tool a question. The system produces words that address the question in a coherent and often accurate way. Is it understanding the question, or is it producing the text that most closely matches what an answer to this question would look like, based on patterns from training?

In many cases, the distinction does not matter practically. If the output is accurate and useful, it serves your purpose.

But in some cases, it matters a great deal. A system that genuinely understands a question can tell you when the question is based on a false assumption, when important context is missing, or when the question cannot be answered without additional information. A system that is pattern-matching to produce a plausible answer will often produce that answer without flagging these issues, because producing an apparently plausible answer is what it was trained to do.

This is why treating AI outputs as starting points for your own thinking, rather than as conclusions, remains important regardless of how impressive those outputs become.

What People Usually Get Wrong the First Time

Most people, when they first seriously engage with AI, make one of two opposite mistakes. The first is thinking it is magic. The second is thinking it is just autocomplete.

Neither is accurate, and both lead to frustration. The magic view leads to disappointment when the AI confidently says something wrong or fails at a task that seems obvious. If it can write a poem in the style of Shakespeare, how can it not know what day it is? The answer is that these abilities come from completely different things. Writing like Shakespeare is a pattern it encountered thousands of times in training. Knowing today's date is a fact that changes every day and was not in the training data.

The autocomplete view leads to underestimating what AI can do. Modern language models do something more interesting than finishing sentences. They have processed such an enormous breadth of human knowledge, reasoning, and expression that they can connect ideas across domains, explain complex concepts in different ways, find analogies, and generate useful content across an enormous range of tasks. That is meaningfully more than a phone keyboard suggesting the next word.

The right mental model is somewhere between the two: a system of remarkable breadth and speed, with specific and predictable limitations. The more accurately you hold this model, the more consistently useful AI becomes.

A Good Starting Question

When you encounter any AI application, in any context, one question cuts through most of the confusion: what specific task is this doing, and what kind of data was it trained to do that task?

A medical AI that helps detect diabetic retinopathy was trained on hundreds of thousands of labelled eye scans. That is a narrow task with a large, well-labelled dataset. It is reasonable to expect it to perform well in conditions like its training data.

A general language model was trained on an enormous variety of texts. It is reasonable to expect it to handle a wide range of language tasks reasonably well. It is not reasonable to expect it to have current information, perfect factual accuracy, or reliable performance on tasks very different from what appears in human-written text.

The question of what task and what data tells you almost everything you need to know about how much to trust any AI system for any particular purpose.

CHAPTER SUMMARY

- AI finds patterns in data and uses those patterns to make predictions. Everything else is a variation on this one idea.
- AI, Machine Learning, and Deep Learning are nested concepts: each is a more specific subset of the previous.
- AI arrived when data, computing power, and a key 2017 architectural breakthrough (the transformer) converged simultaneously.
- AI excels at image recognition, language tasks, and prediction from historical data. It struggles with

common sense, knowing when it is wrong, and ethical judgment.

- The intelligence in artificial intelligence is real but narrow. Knowing this is the foundation for using it well.

CHAPTER TWO

How AI Learns to Be Smart

The surprisingly simple idea behind remarkably powerful machines.

If you asked a child to learn arithmetic by giving them one million worked examples with no explanations, no rules, no teacher, and asking them to figure out the underlying pattern by themselves, you would expect failure. Human learning does not work that way.

This is approximately how AI learns. And at sufficient scale, with the right architecture and enough computing power, it works remarkably well. Understanding the training process does not require mathematics or programming knowledge. It requires only a willingness to follow an idea through to its conclusion.

Learning from Examples: The Core Idea

Every AI system that does something useful learned to do it from data. Not from instructions. Not from rules written by a programmer. From examples.

A spam filter learned what spam looks like by seeing thousands of labelled spam emails alongside thousands of legitimate ones. A medical imaging system learned to identify abnormalities by processing hundreds of thousands of scans labelled by expert radiologists. A language tool learned to write coherent text by processing an enormous amount of human-written text and learning what typically follows what.

The result of this process is called a model. Think of a model as a very complex set of learned preferences, billions of small adjustments that together produce useful behavior. The model does not contain rules. It contains patterns in a mathematical form that are difficult to interpret even for the people who built it. This is one reason AI systems can sometimes do things that surprise even their creators.

The process of creating a model from data is called training.

Three Ways AI Learns

Supervised Learning: The Labelled Examples Method

Supervised learning is the most common approach and the most intuitive. You provide the AI with a large collection of examples that have already been labelled with the correct answer, and the system learns to produce correct answers for new, unlabeled examples.

Consider an email spam filter. Someone collects a large set of emails and labels for each one: spam or not spam. The AI trains on this labelled collection, learning the patterns that distinguish one category from the other. After training, it classifies new emails it has never seen based on the patterns it discovered.

Most of the AI you interact with daily runs on supervised learning. Image recognition, fraud detection, voice transcription, medical diagnosis support: all trained with labelled examples.

Unsupervised Learning: Finding Hidden Structure

Unsupervised learning gives the AI data with no labels at all. No correct answers. Just raw examples and instructions to find whatever structure might exist in them.

This has a crucial advantage: unlabeled data is vastly more abundant than labelled data. Labelling data requires human time and expertise. Unsupervised approaches can work with the unlabeled majority.

Unsupervised learning is how recommendation systems discover that customers who buy certain combinations of products also tend to buy other specific products. Nobody told the system this; it found the grouping by looking for patterns in raw purchase data.

Think of it like sorting a huge pile of mixed items without any categories given to you in advance. You would naturally start grouping things that seem similar. Unsupervised learning does something analogous to data.

Reinforcement Learning: The Trial and Error Method

Reinforcement learning is conceptually the closest to how animals and humans learn through experience. The AI takes action, receives feedback on whether that action was good or bad, and over time learns to take actions that lead to better outcomes.

This is how AI systems learned to play games at superhuman levels. DeepMind's AlphaGo learned to play the board game Go by playing millions of games against itself, receiving a reward for winning and adjusting its strategy accordingly. It started knowing almost nothing about Go strategy. Through sheer repetition at an extraordinary scale, it discovered strategies that surprised even the world's top players.

Reinforcement learning is also used to refine language tools after initial training. Human evaluators rate responses for quality, and the model uses those ratings as a reward signal to adjust toward producing responses that humans find more helpful and appropriate.

Supervised Learning — *learns from labelled examples.*

Unsupervised Learning — *finds hidden patterns.*

Reinforcement Learning — *learns from feedback.*

Figure 2.1: Three Ways AI Learns: Supervised, Unsupervised, Reinforcement

The Training Process in Practice

Training a large AI model is a significant undertaking. Understanding what it involves helps explain why powerful AI systems exist now when they did not before.

The process begins with the model's weights set to random values. The model knows nothing. The training data, which might be billions of examples, is fed through the model in batches. For each batch, the model makes predictions, the predictions are compared to the correct answers, and the difference is used to calculate how to adjust the weights.

The measure of how wrong the model is at any given moment is called the loss. High loss means the model is far from correct. Low loss means it is close. The process of adjusting weights to reduce the loss is called gradient descent.

Over time, the loss decreases. The model becomes less wrong. After sufficient training, the real test is whether the model performs well on data it has never seen before, not just on the training data. This distinction matters enormously.

Training a frontier language model currently requires enormous computing resources, significant time, and costs that run into tens of millions of dollars. This is one reason only a small number of organizations in the world can train the most powerful models from scratch.

A Real Story: The Protein Folding Problem

For roughly fifty years, one of the hardest problems in biology was predicting the three-dimensional shape of proteins from their chemical sequence. Proteins do their work by folding into specific shapes, and knowing those shapes is crucial for understanding disease and developing treatments. Determining a single protein shape by experimental methods could take years of laboratory work.

In 2020, DeepMind released Alpha Fold, a system that could predict protein shapes with accuracy far beyond anything that had come before. In 2022, they released predictions for essentially every protein in the human body and hundreds of millions of proteins across other organisms, creating a freely available database that researchers worldwide could use immediately.

This is a real example of AI doing something that matters. Researchers who spent careers working out the shapes of individual proteins now had access to predictions for millions of them. Drug development timelines have shortened. Research directions that had been too slow to pursue became feasible.

The system had no grasp of what a protein does inside a living cell; no sense of what the discovery meant for human health. It identified structural regularities in a large dataset and generalized from them. The scientific significance was entirely a human interpretation layered on top. Pattern recognition at an extraordinary scale, applied to a problem that had resisted human effort for half a century.

Story: A Fifty-Year Problem, Then a Free Database

When DeepMind released the AlphaFold protein structure database in 2022, something happened that the researchers had not fully anticipated. Within weeks, scientists in countries that had never had access to expensive laboratory equipment were downloading the data and starting work.

A research team in Kenya working on malaria proteins had spent years trying to understand the structure of specific proteins that the malaria parasite uses to evade the immune system. The experimental work needed to determine protein structures takes months and specialized equipment that most labs in the developing world simply do not have. With AlphaFold's predictions, they could start working with structural data the same week the database went live.

A group of researchers studying neglected tropical diseases, illnesses that affect hundreds of millions of people in low-income countries but receive comparatively little pharmaceutical investment, found that they could now pursue research directions that had previously been too slow and too expensive to attempt.

This is worth pausing on. The AlphaFold system was trained on decades of accumulated protein structure data from labs around the world. The training process required enormous computing resources. The result was made freely available to any researcher anywhere with an internet connection.

The AI did not set out to help anyone. It had no goals. But the decision to release the outputs openly meant that a tool built with significant resources became accessible to people who had none of those resources. The work being done on the back of it is real. Some of it may lead somewhere important for diseases that have not had enough attention.

This is one of the more quietly significant things that has happened in science in recent years. It did not make many headlines outside specialist circles. But its effects are ongoing.

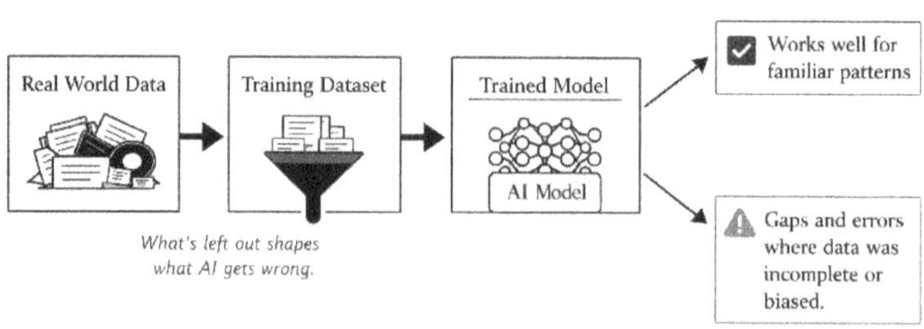

Figure 2.2: How Training Data Shapes What AI Knows and Gets Wrong

Why AI Fails: The Data Problem

Every significant limitation of AI systems traces back, in one way or another, to the data they were trained on.

The most fundamental issue is called distribution shift: the gap between the data the AI was trained on and the data it encounters in the real world. An AI trained on medical scans from hospitals in one region may perform worse on scans from hospitals elsewhere that use different equipment or serve populations with different characteristics. The world changes; training data does not update itself.

Critically, the AI has no way of knowing when it is outside its training distribution. It continues making predictions with the same apparent confidence whether it is in familiar territory or far outside it. The absence of uncertainty signals is not the same as accuracy.

The second major data problem is that training data encodes the biases, errors, and limitations of whoever and whatever created it. If the historical data used to train a hiring system reflects past patterns of who was hired, the system will learn those patterns, including any unfair ones. If the medical literature used to train a diagnostic system over-represents certain populations, the system may perform worse for populations that appear less frequently.

These are not bugs in the traditional sense. They are features of learning from data. The data reflects the world; the AI learns what the data reflects.

The Difference Between Memorizing and Learning

A model that has only been memorized will perform well on training examples and poorly on everything else. This is called overfitting: the model has fitted itself so tightly to its training data that it cannot generalize. The equivalent in human learning would be a student who memorizes the exact questions from last year's exam without understanding the underlying subject.

A well-known example: researchers trained an AI to distinguish images of wolves from images of dogs. The system achieved high accuracy on test data. When they examined which features it was using, they found it had largely learned to use the background. Wolves appeared in snowy wilderness settings, dogs in domestic ones. The system had not learned to recognize wolves. It had learned to recognize snow.

This kind of failure is difficult to detect in advance. The system performs correctly in testing and only reveals its limitations in edge cases. In low-stakes situations this is inconvenient. In high-stakes applications it can be dangerous.

The Scale That Makes the Difference

When people first learn how AI learns, a natural question arises: surely learning from examples without any explanation of why things are right or wrong must produce fragile results?

The answer is scale. Training datasets for modern AI systems are so large, and the number of training iterations so vast, that the system has encountered an enormous number of versions of each pattern from many different angles.

Think about how a child learns to recognize their faces. They see thousands of faces over years of experience, in many lighting conditions, at different distances, with different expressions. Through all of this exposure, they build a robust internal model of what a face is. An AI image recognition system is trained on millions of face images across millions of variations. Scale is what makes the learned patterns robust and generalizable.

The Hidden Labor Behind the Data

There is a part of AI development that receives relatively little attention in popular discussion: the enormous amount of human labor that goes into creating training data.

For supervised learning, someone must label examples. This work can be tedious, time-consuming, and requires human judgment. For a medical imaging system, expert radiologists need to annotate thousands or millions of scans. For a language tool that aims to produce helpful responses, human evaluators need to assess and rate large numbers of outputs. For a translation system, bilingual speakers need to verify the quality of translated examples.

This work is done by many people, often in arrangements that receive far less attention than the end products. The final AI product looks polished and automated. The labelling work that made it possible is usually invisible.

This is not a reason to avoid using AI tools. It is a reason to have a complete picture of what AI development involves, and to be curious about the conditions under which the training data behind any given system was produced.

What Happens When You Use a Model

Most people who use AI tools are not using models trained from scratch. They are using models that were trained by the organizations that developed them, then made available for use.

When you use a language tool, you are interacting with a model that was trained on a very large amount of text over a long period, using significant computational resources. The model has been further refined to follow instructions, maintain a helpful tone, and avoid certain types of outputs. You are using the result of that entire process through an interface designed to make the interaction simple.

Understanding this helps clarify what you can and cannot expect. The model's knowledge comes from its training data, which has a cutoff date. It does not update itself with new information between conversations. Each conversation typically starts fresh, without memory of previous ones unless a specific feature has been enabled.

The model's capabilities and limitations are fixed at the time of training. You cannot make a language model better at mathematics by asking it to try harder. You can ask it to use different approaches to a mathematical problem, which may produce better results, but the underlying capability is determined by training.

Story: Fifty Milliseconds Between You and a Fraud

Priya is a software consultant in Bengaluru. On a Tuesday morning in 2024, she tapped her phone to pay for an auto-rickshaw fare through UPI. The transaction was completed in under two seconds. What she did not see was a decision that had already been made about her, silently, in the time it took her thumb to leave the screen.

In those fifty milliseconds, a machine learning model examined the transaction against a detailed history of her payment behavior. It knew the kinds of merchants she typically paid, the times of day she usually transacted, the approximate location she was in, the amounts she typically sent, and how all those factors compared to the patterns of hundreds of millions of other UPI users. It had also looked at whether the receiving account had been flagged in connection with any suspicious activity by other users. It weighed all of this simultaneously and produced a risk score. The transaction was ordinary. It was approved without a second thought.

Now consider what happens when the pattern breaks. In the same week, a fraudster in a different city used a compromised phone number to attempt a large transfer to an account that had been associated with previous fraud complaints. The model recognized several signals at once: the account was new, the amount was unusual for that user profile, the transaction was attempted at an odd hour, and the destination had a risk history. The transaction was blocked before it was completed. No human reviewed it. No humans needed to.

The National Payments Corporation of India, which operates UPI, processes over fifteen billion transactions a month. That is not a number any team of human fraud analysts could review in real time. The only way to manage fraud at that volume is with a system that has been trained on enormous amounts of labelled historical data: this transaction was fraud, this one was not, here are the signals that distinguish them. Given enough examples, the model learns to generalize. It can recognize fraud patterns it has never seen in exactly that form because they resemble patterns it has seen before.

This is supervised learning working at the scale of daily Indian life. The model did not have a rule that said fraud looks like this. It was shown millions of examples of what fraud looked like across many different contexts and learned to distinguish it from legitimate transactions. Every time a fraud analyst reviews a flagged transaction and updates the classification, that outcome becomes part of the next round of training. The system improves continuously, fed by real-world results.

The reason this story matters is what it demonstrates about the reach of machine learning. The system protecting your UPI payment is not a piece of software that someone wrote by thinking carefully about fraud and encoding those thoughts as rules. It is the result of pattern recognition applied to the collective behavior of hundreds of millions of people. It is supervised learning at scale, and it is working, quietly, every time you tap your phone.

A Story: Learning Through Repetition at Scale

One of the most striking demonstrations of how AI learns from examples comes from the world of games. DeepMind's AlphaGo Zero, a successor to AlphaGo, was trained to play Go with no human game data at all. It started from scratch, knowing only the rules of the game, and played against itself millions of times.

Within days of training, it had surpassed all previous AI Go programs. Within a few weeks, it had surpassed AlphaGo, which had itself defeated the world champion. It discovered strategies that human players had never used in centuries of Go history.

The lesson is not that AI is cleverer than humans. It is that repeated experience at a scale impossible for humans, combined with clear feedback on outcomes, can produce highly effective behavior even without anything resembling prior knowledge or understanding.

What You Cannot Know About a Model

When you interact with an AI tool, there is much you cannot know about the model you are using. You typically do not know precisely what data it was trained on, what biases or gaps that data contained, what specific refinements were applied after initial training, or what its known failure modes are.

The organizations developing the most powerful models have been increasingly publishing research and documentation about their systems, but even the most detailed documentation does not give a complete picture of everything that shapes a model's behavior.

This asymmetry is important to hold in mind. The model's capabilities and limitations are determined by processes you cannot fully observe. The appropriate response is consistent critical engagement with outputs, rather than blanket trust or blanket distrust. Calibrate your trust based on experience with the system, the stakes of the task, and your ability to verify outputs independently.

What a Model Actually Is

After training, what you are left with is a model. That word gets used constantly in AI discussion, so it is worth being clear about what it actually means.

A model is the result of the training process: a very large set of numbers, billions of them for a large language model, adjusted through training so that when information flows through the mathematical structure they define, the right kind of output comes out the other side.

You cannot open a model and read what it has learned the way you might read a book. Knowledge is not stored as facts or rules. It is distributed across billions of numerical values in a way that has no clean human-readable interpretation. Even the people who built the model cannot fully explain why it produces any particular output. This is sometimes called the black box problem, and it is a genuine challenge for understanding AI systems and debugging them when they go wrong.

The useful analogy is to your own brain. You know how to ride a bicycle. But you cannot explain the specific neural patterns that let you do it. The knowledge is there; it works, but it is not stored in a form you can inspect directly. AI models have an analogous property, except that at least in principle someone could look at the numbers. In practice, with hundreds of billions of parameters, the numbers do not tell you much at the human level.

This is partly why AI can surprise even its creators. The training process is well understood. What exactly emerges from it, at the level of specific capabilities and limitations, is not always fully predictable in advance.

The Difference Between a Small and a Large Model

Not all AI models are the same size, and size matters in specific ways.

A small model, perhaps with millions of parameters, can be run on a phone or a cheap computer. It performs well on narrow, specific tasks. A model trained to recognize specific types of manufacturing defects on a production line can be small and fast and accurate for exactly that task.

A large model, with hundreds of billions of parameters, requires significant computing infrastructure to run. It can handle a much wider range of tasks and is more capable at complex reasoning, nuanced language, and cross-domain knowledge. But it is also more expensive to run and produces answers more slowly than a small specialist model.

Most of the AI tools that people use in daily life are powered by large models hosted in data centers and accessed over the internet. The AI assistant on your phone for local processing tasks, like on-device voice recognition, typically runs on smaller models designed to work with limited computing resources.

Neither is better in general. The right size depends on the task, the constraints, and the trade-offs involved.

CHAPTER SUMMARY

- AI learns from examples through training: showing a model data, measuring how wrong it is, and making billions of small adjustments.
- Three learning approaches: supervised (labelled examples), unsupervised (finding hidden structure), reinforcement (trial and reward).
- Neural networks are layers of simple mathematical operations that, combined at enormous scale, produce sophisticated capability.
- DeepMind's AlphaFold (2020) predicted the structure of essentially every known protein, a fifty-year biology problem. This is a documented real-world example of AI impact.
- All AI limitations trace back to data: distribution shift, embedded bias, and the difference between memorizing and genuinely learning are the core failure modes.

CHAPTER THREE

How to Talk to AI

The skill nobody teaches you, but everybody needs.

There is a version of you that opens a language tool, types a vague question, gets a mediocre answer, and concludes that AI is not that useful. There is another version of you that types a specific, well-framed question, gets a genuinely helpful response, and saves an hour of work. The difference between those two experiences is not the AI. It is whether you know how to communicate with it effectively.

This skill is called prompting. No technical background is required. You are writing in plain language. But there are principles to how you write that make an enormous difference to what you get back.

What a Prompt Actually Is

A prompt is simply everything you type into an AI language tool. Your instruction, your question, your request, any context you provide. The AI reads your prompt and generates a response based on everything it has learned during training, filtered through what your prompt tells it about what you need.

Most people treat AI like a search engine. They type a few keywords and expect good results. Search engines are built to handle vague queries. Language tools are not search engines. They are more like a capable colleague who knows nothing about your specific situation and can only work with what you tell them.

A prompt is closer to a brief you give to a capable new assistant. The more clearly you explain the situation, what you need, and what the output should look like, the better the result. They cannot read your mind. Neither can the AI.

If you get a poor result, the most useful question to ask is not what is wrong with this AI but rather what could I have explained more clearly. Often the answer is apparent once you ask the question.

The Four Components of a Good Prompt

Good prompts tend to have four components. You do not need all four every time. For a simple question, one or two is enough. For a complex task, all four make the difference between a useful result and a frustrating one.

Role: Tell the AI Who to Be

AI language tools respond differently depending on the perspective you ask them to take. If you ask for an explanation with no context, the tool will guess at the appropriate level. If you specify who you want it to be, it calibrates accordingly.

Without role: "Explain how vaccines work." With role: "You are a science teacher explaining to a group of twelve-year-olds. Explain how vaccines work using examples they would find familiar."

The second version produces a fundamentally different response, not because the AI knows more, but because you gave it a clear target.

Context: Tell the AI Your Situation

The AI knows nothing about you unless you say so. Context makes the difference between a generic answer and a useful one.

Without context: "Help me write a message to my manager." With context: "I am a junior employee at a software company. I need to tell my manager that I will miss a deadline because of unexpected technical problems. I want to be professional and honest without sounding like I am making excuses."

The second request can produce a useful draft.

Task: Be Specific About What You Want

Vague requests produce vague results.

Vague: "Help me with my presentation." Specific: "I have a ten-minute presentation for my department about why we should update our customer feedback process. I have four slides and I think the third one is too complicated. Can you suggest simpler ways to explain the same idea?"

Format: Tell the AI How to Respond

You can specify exactly how you want the response structured. Ask for a numbered list and you will get one. Ask for a short paragraph and you will get one. If you do not specify, the AI will choose, and its default is often more text than you needed.

Simple format instructions that work: "Keep the answer to three sentences." Or: "Give me a bulleted list of the most important points." Or: "Give me the answer first, then the explanation."

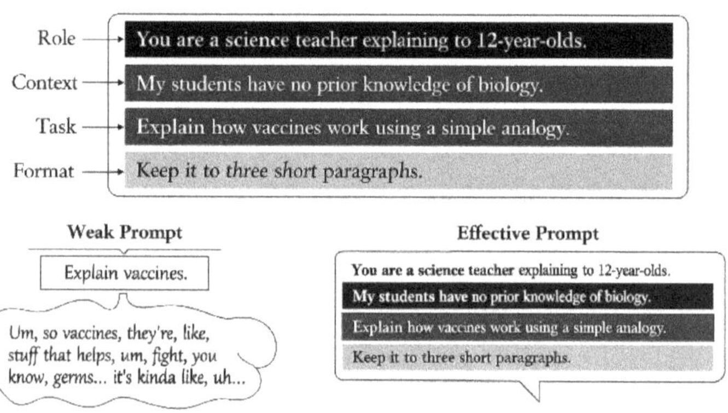

Figure 3.1: The Four Components of an Effective Prompt

Seeing the Difference: Before and After

Getting Help with a Difficult Conversation

Weak: "How do I tell someone bad news?" Strong: "I am a team lead, and I need to tell one of my team members that they did not get a promotion they expected. They have been working hard and I know they will be disappointed. I want to be honest and kind. How should I approach this conversation, and what should I say when they ask why?"

The strong version produces a practical, situation-specific guide that accounts for the emotional dynamics, the professional context, and the specific difficult moment you flagged.

Making Sense of Something Complex

Weak: "Explain interest rates." Strong: "Explain how interest rates affect a home loan for someone who has a fixed-rate mortgage they took out three years ago and is now hearing news about central banks raising rates. Do they need to worry about their existing loan?"

The strong version answers your actual question with enough explanation to help you understand why, without unnecessary complexity.

Learning a New Skill

Weak: "How do I get better at public speaking?" Strong: "I am comfortable in small meetings but I freeze up when presenting to groups of more than ten people. I have a presentation to thirty people in three weeks. What are the two or three most effective things I can focus on in the time I have, given that my main problem is anxiety rather than lack of knowledge?"

The strong version gives targeted, prioritized guidance that addresses your actual constraint and works within your timeframe.

The Most Important Skill: Iteration

Most guides about prompting do not tell you this clearly enough: your first prompt does not need to be perfect. Treating it as a draft and iterating is the most important habit to develop.

When you get a response that is not quite what you wanted, do not start over. Tell the AI specifically what to change. "That was helpful but too formal." Or: "Can you make the explanation shorter?" Or: "I liked that structure but I need more focus on the financial aspects."

Think of it as a conversation rather than a single transaction. People who use AI tools regularly often describe spending several exchanges refining a single output until it is right. This is not a sign that the tool is not working. It is the normal pattern of getting something useful out of a complex task.

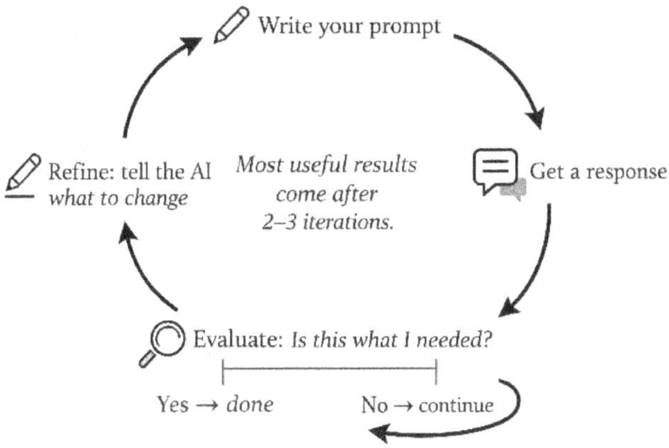

Figure 3.2: The Prompt Iteration Loop

Practical Templates You Can Adapt

For understanding something complex: You are explaining to someone who has a general education but no specialist knowledge of this field. Explain [topic] clearly, starting with the most important idea, using concrete examples.

For getting feedback on your writing: Read this piece of writing and give me specific, constructive feedback. I want to know: what is the strongest part, what is the weakest part, and what one change would most improve it. Be direct.

For preparing for a difficult conversation: I need to have a conversation with [description of person and relationship] about [topic]. The key challenge is [specific difficulty]. Help me think through how to approach this, what to say, and what their likely responses might be.

For summarizing long material: Summarize the key points of the following in [number] bullet points. Focus on [specific aspect if relevant]. Then tell me the single most important idea.

These templates demonstrate the principle: role, context, task, format. The more precisely you fill in each component for your actual situation, the more useful the result.

What AI Cannot Fix

AI language tools are not reliable sources for factual information that requires current accuracy. The tools are trained up to a certain date and do not update themselves. If you ask about recent events, current prices, or the latest research, you may receive outdated or invented information presented with apparent confidence. Always verify time-sensitive or consequential facts through current sources.

AI is not reliable for high-stakes professional decisions. For matters affecting your health, legal rights, or significant amounts of money, AI output is a starting point for your own thinking, not a substitute for advice from a qualified professional who understands your specific situation.

AI cannot verify its own outputs. It can tell you confidently what sounds right based on patterns in its training data, but it has no mechanism for distinguishing between something it knows to be true and something it generated that sounds plausible. This is the hallucination problem again. Bring your own critical thinking to every interaction.

A Real Story: The Lawyer and the Fake Cases

In 2023, a legal case in a New York court attracted widespread attention when it emerged that a lawyer had submitted a legal brief citing several court cases as precedents. The judge asked for copies of those cases. They did not exist. The lawyer had used an AI language tool to help prepare the brief. The tool had generated case citations that sounded completely plausible and real but were entirely fabricated.

The story was reported widely as a cautionary tale. The more useful lesson is specific: AI language tools can generate text with the form and style of accurate information while the content is invented. In a domain where accuracy is non-negotiable, the failure to verify AI outputs had serious professional and legal consequences.

This does not mean language tools are useless for legal or professional work. Many professionals use them productively every day. It means the tools are not substitutes for expertise and verification. They are assistants, not authorities.

Developing Your Own Prompting Sense

The principles in this chapter will improve your results immediately. Over time, you will develop an intuitive sense for when to add more context, when to specify a role, when to push back and ask for something different.

A useful question to ask yourself before submitting a prompt: if a capable but completely uninformed colleague received this request with no other context, what would they need to know to give me a useful response? Add whatever the answer reveals.

The people who get the most out of AI tools are not the people who know the most about AI. They are the people who are clearest about what they need and most willing to refine their requests until they get it.

The Difference Between Using AI and Using AI Well

There is a gap between using AI and using AI well that is larger than most people realize when they first start. Closing that gap does not require technical knowledge. It requires the same skills that separate good communication from poor communication in any context: clarity, specificity, and the willingness to engage iteratively rather than expecting perfection on the first attempt.

Most people begin using AI tools the same way they began using search engines: type a few words and see what comes back. For search, this works reasonably well because search engines are designed to handle vague queries and find relevant existing content. Language tools are not doing this. They are generating responses based on what your prompt suggests you need. A vague prompt generates a vague response. A specific prompt generates a specific response.

This skill develops quickly with practice. People who use language tools regularly tend to describe a rapid improvement in their results within the first few weeks, not because the tools changed but because they developed better instincts for how to frame requests.

When AI Surprises You

Occasional surprising outputs are a feature of language AI that experienced users learn to navigate productively.

Sometimes the AI will produce something better than what you asked for: an angle you had not considered, a way of expressing an idea that is clearer than what you had in mind. When this happens, resist the reflex to simply move on. Ask yourself whether the surprising element is actually valuable, and if it is, incorporate it.

Sometimes the AI will produce something that is confidently wrong in an interesting way. It will assert something false, use an example that does not work, or apply a concept in a way that reveals a misunderstanding. When this happens, it is worth investigating whether the error is consistent or isolated. Ask the same question in a different way. The answer will tell you something about the reliability of the AI in this particular domain.

Sometimes the AI will misunderstand what you meant. This is almost always the result of ambiguity in the prompt. The most efficient response is to identify the specific ambiguity and rephrase. Saying the output was not what I needed is less useful than saying you interpreted my request as X, but I actually meant Y.

Treating surprises as information rather than frustrations tends to make the whole experience calmer and more useful.

The Limits of Personalization

AI language tools can simulate personalization based on what you tell them in the current conversation. If you describe your background, your preferences, and your situation, the AI can tailor its responses accordingly. This can be useful.

But this personalisation is surface-level in an important sense. The AI does not know you. It has no history with you unless specific memory features are enabled. It cannot tell that the way you phrased a question suggests you are having a difficult day, or that the question you are asking has implications you have not mentioned.

Human experts develop knowledge of their clients, students, or patients over time that shapes how they interact. They remember what worked and what did not. They can detect when something is off. They build a relationship that makes their advice more valuable over time.

AI tools, as typically used, cannot do this. Each conversation is largely a fresh start. This means the quality of what you get depends heavily on what you put in. Give context every time. Do not assume the AI remembers what you told it before. Think of each conversation as a briefing, not a continuation.

Prompting Mistakes Worth Avoiding

A few common mistakes reduce the quality of AI responses and are easy to fix once you are aware of them.

Asking too many things at once is perhaps the most common. If you have five questions, ask them one at a time or in clearly separated groups. An AI given five things to address in one prompt often handles none of them as well as it would handle each one individually.

Being passive in follow-up is another. Many people accept a response that is almost but not quite right rather than telling the AI specifically what to change. The fix is to be direct: this is too formal; this missed the point, make the third paragraph shorter, focus more on the cost implications. Specific feedback produces specific improvements.

Assuming the AI has context, it does not have is a third common mistake. If you started a related conversation two days ago, the AI does not remember it. If you are asking a follow-up question, provide the context of what came before. The AI is not tracking your project. You are.

CHAPTER SUMMARY

- A good prompt has four components: a role for the AI, context about your situation, a specific task, and a format instruction.
- The most important prompting habit is iteration: treat the first response as a draft and refine from there.
- AI is unreliable for time-sensitive facts, high-stakes professional advice, and tasks requiring verified accuracy.
- In 2023, a lawyer in New York submitted a legal brief citing fabricated case references generated by an AI tool. It is a clear illustration of what happens when AI outputs go unverified.

CHAPTER FOUR

AI in Your Pocket

It was already everywhere. You just did not notice.

Before AI became a topic of constant conversation, it was already a constant presence. It was in the phone you carried, the feed you scrolled, the map you consulted, the bank fraud alert you received, the playlist that somehow knew exactly what you wanted to hear. You did not notice most of it because it was designed to be seamless.

This chapter maps the AI that already exists in your daily life. Not to make you feel uneasy, though some of what you find here may prompt reflection, but because understanding what is already present is the foundation for thinking clearly about what comes next.

A Day in the Life: AI from 6 AM to Midnight

The easiest way to understand how thoroughly AI has been woven into daily life is not to explain it in the abstract but to follow one ordinary day. What follows is the story of Meera, a marketing manager in Mumbai. Nothing unusual happens to Meera on this day. That is precisely the point.

Morning

At 6:14 AM, Meera's phone wakes her. She did not set an alarm for 6:14. She set it for 6:30, but her phone's sleep-tracking feature, which uses the accelerometer to monitor her movement through the night, detected that she was already in a light sleep phase and that waking her now would be gentler than waking her in the deeper phase she would likely be in at 6:30. This is a small AI decision with a small benefit. She is not particularly grateful for it. She does not know it happened.

She checks her messages. Her email application has sorted her inbox automatically. Promotional messages are in a separate folder. The important emails are at the top, ranked by a model that has observed which senders and subject lines she typically opens quickly. A newsletter she subscribed to three months ago and has not opened since has been quietly moved to a promotions tab. She does not notice its absence.

She opens a news application. Every headline she sees has been selected by a recommendation algorithm that knows which topics she clicks on, how long she spends reading certain types of stories, and what users with similar reading patterns have been engaging with. The news is real. But the selection of which news she sees first is not neutral. It reflects a model's prediction of what will hold her attention.

In the kitchen, she asks her voice assistant to add items to her shopping list. The voice recognition system converts her spoken words to text with an accuracy that would have seemed remarkable a decade ago, trained on hundreds of thousands of hours of speech in multiple Indian accents and languages. The music it plays during her morning routine was chosen by an algorithm that has noted her listening patterns for years: the tempo she tends to prefer before 8 AM, the artists she skips, the genres she returns to.

The Commute

Before leaving, Meera checks a navigation application for traffic updates. The application knows her usual route. It also knows that a stretch of road near the station was congested yesterday at this time, that it is slightly congested right now based on real-time signals from other users' phones in the area, and that at her current pace she will arrive at the station four minutes before her usual train. It recommends a small variation to her route that saves two minutes. She follows it without thinking about where the suggestion came from.

On the train, she opens a short video platform and watches three videos during the fifteen-minute journey. Each one was selected by a recommendation model. The first was from a creator she follows. The second was from a creator she has never seen before, whose style and topic pattern closely resembles the creators she engages with most. The third was a sponsored post, placed there because her profile matches the advertiser's target audience. She watches all three. The algorithm notes this and adjusts its model of her preferences accordingly.

Story: The Waitlist That Knew You Were Getting a Seat

Anyone who has booked a train ticket through IRCTC has encountered one of the more emotionally charged AI interactions in Indian daily life: the waitlist. You book a ticket, receive a status like WL 34 or WL 12, and then something happens that feels almost mysterious. Some waitlists clear quickly. Some stay stuck and then move suddenly in the last forty-eight hours before departure. Some never clear at all.

What looks like mystery is actually a prediction system working with an enormous amount of historical data.

Indian Railways moves roughly twenty-three million passengers every day across more than thirteen thousand trains. The waitlist clearance system draws on years of booking records: which routes have high cancellation rates, at what point before departure those cancellations tend to cluster, which travel classes are most likely to free up seats, how current demand for this route compares to historical demand for this date and season.

When a travel agent tells you confidently that your WL 8 on the Mumbai-Delhi Rajdhani will clear, they are doing an informal version of what the model does formally: matching the current situation against similar historical situations. The difference is that the model has processed millions of such situations rather than hundreds.

The dynamic pricing on premium trains like Shatabdi and Vande Bharat works on related principles. The fare you see for a specific date reflects a demand prediction model assessing how many seats will sell at different price points, based on the date, route, time until departure, and historical booking velocity. Prices adjust as bookings accumulate and the model updates its prediction of remaining demand.

The next time you watch your PNR status refresh and wonder whether your waitlist will move, you are watching a prediction system built on decades of travel data from hundreds of millions of Indian journeys. It is not always right. But it is making an informed estimate, not a guess, and the difference between those two things is exactly what machine learning is for.

Story: What Twenty-Eight Minutes Actually Means

When a food delivery application shows you an estimated arrival time of twenty-eight minutes, that number did not come from a human dispatcher looking at a map. It came from a model simultaneously weighing the restaurant's current order queue, its historical preparation time for the items you ordered, the location and movement speed of available delivery partners, real-time traffic conditions on likely routes, weather data, and demand patterns on the platform at this specific time of day.

Meera's colleague Vikram orders delivery almost every working day. He has noticed that on Friday afternoons estimates are consistently longer than on weekday mornings, and that during major cricket matches the estimates become noticeably unreliable. He finds this mildly frustrating. He has not thought carefully about why it happens.

The reason is one of the most important concepts in understanding where AI goes wrong: distribution shift. The delivery model was trained on historical data. It knows what a normal Friday afternoon looks like with high confidence because it has seen thousands of them. But a Friday afternoon during the final of a major tournament, with an unusual spike in orders from people watching at home and fewer delivery partners on the road, sits outside the range of situations the model has seen in that exact combination. When the real world differs significantly from the patterns in the training data, the model's predictions degrade.

Vikram calls this Swiggy being slow during the World Cup. Data scientists call it distribution shift. They are describing exactly the same thing.

This matters beyond the inconvenience of a late lunch. The same principle explains why a fraud detection model may perform less accurately during a festival season when spending patterns shift, why a medical AI trained on one population may be less reliable for a different demographic group, and why any AI system deployed in the real world needs to be monitored for changes in the environment it was trained on. The lesson from a delayed biryani turns out to generalize quite far.

Evening and Night

On the commute home, Meera uses a ride-hailing application. The fare was calculated by a model assessing current demand in her zone, available driver supply nearby, predicted demand over the next twenty minutes, and the expected travel time. The driver matched to her was selected by an algorithm weighing proximity, ratings, route efficiency, and the driver's own preference settings. Neither she nor the driver made the match. The system did.

At home, she watches a streaming series that the service recommended to her three times over the past two weeks before she tried it. The recommendation was based on the watch history of users with patterns similar to hers. She enjoys it. This is another data point that reinforces the model's confidence in recommendations for users with her profile.

Before sleeping, she checks her banking application. A transaction she made that afternoon has been flagged with a notification asking her to confirm it was intentional: a first-time purchase at an unfamiliar merchant in an unusual category. She confirms it. The model notes that this type of transaction is acceptable for her. She dismisses the notification and does not think about it again.

Meera's day was entirely ordinary. She made no decisions about technology. She did not opt in to anything consciously or engage with AI deliberately. She simply lived her life. In doing so, she interacted with machine learning systems forty or fifty times: in navigation, communication, entertainment, food, transport, finance, and work. Most interactions improved something slightly. A few shaped her choices in ways she was not aware of. None of them announced themselves.

This is the actual texture of AI in daily life. Not a transformation that arrived with a headline but a dense, quiet presence in the infrastructure of ordinary decisions, already so familiar that most people do not notice it is there at all.

Your Phone: An AI Device That Also Makes Calls

The camera on a modern smartphone is perhaps the most accessible demonstration of AI in everyday life. When you point your camera at a face, the phone identifies the face, distinguishes it from the background, adjusts focus and exposure specifically for it, and in some cases recognizes whose face it is if you have a photo library. None of this involves rules written by a programmer specifying what a face looks like. All of it involves models trained on enormous numbers of photographs.

When you speak to your phone to set a timer or send a message by voice, the system converting your speech to text is an AI model trained on hundreds of thousands of hours of human speech in many accents and languages. When you type and the keyboard suggests your next word, a language model trained on text patterns is making that suggestion. When you search your photo library for "beach" and it finds beach photographs you never labelled, an image recognition model is doing that work.

Translation features, augmented reality that overlays information on camera views, facial recognition that unlocks your device: these are all AI systems operating quietly in the background of something you use dozens of times a day.

Navigation: A Quiet Revolution

Navigation AI is one of the most widely used and least discussed AI applications in everyday life. Modern navigation applications do not just show you a route. They use AI to predict traffic patterns based on current conditions and historical data, reroute you in real time as conditions change, estimate arrival times accurate to within minutes, and identify road incidents from aggregated data from other users.

The accuracy of traffic prediction has improved dramatically as datasets have grown. Earlier navigation systems showed you where traffic was. Modern ones predict where traffic will be when you reach each segment of your route, based on patterns from millions of previous journeys.

For anyone who remembers consulting a printed map before leaving home, the contrast is striking.

The Invisible Recommendations Shaping Your Choices

Recommendation systems are among the most widely deployed AI applications in the world, and among the least visible. They decide what you see when you open a shopping application, a news feed, a streaming service, or a social media platform.

A streaming service recommendation system does not know you personally. It knows your watch history and the watch patterns of millions of other users. It finds users whose patterns are similar to yours and recommends things those users engaged with that you have not seen yet. This works reasonably well much of the time. It also creates feedback loops: the more you watch a certain type of content, the more that type is recommended, and so on. Your preferences can gradually narrow without you being aware of it.

Shopping recommendation systems work similarly but with additional signals. What you searched for. What you viewed but did not buy. What you bought and when. How long you spent looking at particular pages. All of these feed into a model predicting what you are likely to want next.

The recommendations on social platforms are more complex because they are not just predicting what content you will enjoy. They are also optimizing for engagement, meaning the platform's goal is to keep you on the platform as long as possible. Content that provokes strong emotional reactions tends to keep people engaged longer, regardless of whether that reaction is positive or negative. This is not a conspiracy theory; it is the documented result of optimizing for time-on-platform as a metric. Understanding that the curator of your feed has different goals than your own wellbeing is useful context for thinking about your relationship with these platforms.

Financial AI: The Machine Deciding Your Money

Every time you use a bank card, a risk assessment is made almost instantaneously. The system checks your transaction against your history: is this the kind of purchase you typically make, at this kind of merchant, in this location, at this time of day? If something is unusual, the transaction may be flagged or declined. This all happens in milliseconds across millions of transactions without a human reviewing each one. An AI model is doing the assessment.

Credit decisions are increasingly made with AI assistance. When you apply for a credit card or a loan, a score is calculated based on many factors from your credit history. AI models are used both to calculate these scores and to assist in decisions about creditworthiness. The models can identify patterns that traditional scoring systems miss, which can be an advantage. They can also encode historical biases present in past lending decisions, which can be a disadvantage. We will return to this in Chapter Six.

Insurance pricing is another area where AI has become significant. The price you are quoted for car insurance, health insurance, or home insurance may be influenced by AI models assessing risk based on a large number of factors, some of which customers might not expect.

Healthcare AI: Promise and Limitation

Healthcare is one of the areas where AI capabilities and limitations are both most significant. The stakes are high, the potential benefits are real, and the risks of getting things wrong are serious.

On the positive side, AI has demonstrated genuine value in medical imaging. Systems for detecting diabetic retinopathy from eye scans, identifying early signs of certain cancers from imaging, and flagging potential abnormalities in chest scans for radiologist review have all shown accuracy that, in controlled studies, matches or exceeds experienced specialists for specific, well-defined tasks. The key words are specific and well-defined. These are pattern recognition tasks with large training datasets and clear outcomes.

The limitations are equally important. AI diagnostic systems perform well on cases well-represented in their training data and poorly on unusual presentations, rare conditions, and patients who differ significantly from the training population. A system trained primarily on data from one demographic group may perform less accurately for other groups.

AI systems also cannot take a patient history, notice that someone seems frightened or confused, ask the follow-up question prompted by something that does not quite fit the pattern, or exercise the clinical judgment that comes from years of seeing patients as complete human beings. The value of AI in healthcare is as a tool that assists human clinicians, extending their reach and helping them catch things they might miss. Not as a replacement.

Story: A Photograph of a Leaf

Ramesh grows tomatoes on a small farm in Nagpur district. He has been farming for twenty years. In the summer of 2023, he noticed the leaves on several of his plants turning yellow and curling at the edges. He had seen something like it before, but was not sure if it was the same problem he had dealt with years ago or something different.

The nearest agricultural extension officer covers dozens of villages. Getting an in-person visit could mean waiting days, by which point the problem might have spread further.

Ramesh's son had the Plantix app on his phone. He photographed the affected leaf and uploaded it. Within seconds, the app returned a diagnosis: early blight, a fungal disease, with a confidence rating and a set of recommended treatments including both chemical and organic options, all described in Marathi.

They treated the plants that afternoon. The outbreak was contained.

This is not a dramatic story. Nobody's life was saved. But it is a precise illustration of what AI can do when it is trained on the right data and put in the right hands.

In India, there is roughly one agricultural extension officer for every thousand farms. That gap is not going to close quickly. An AI app trained on eight hundred disease types across sixty crops, available on an ordinary smartphone, does not replace the expertise of a trained agronomist. But it gives a farmer access to something much better than nothing, at the moment they actually need it, in the language they actually speak.

Plantix has been used by millions of farmers across India and other parts of Asia and Africa. Most of those farmers have never met an agronomist. The app has not solved agriculture. But for a farmer standing in a field looking at a sick plant, it has changed what the next hour looks like.

A Real Case: The Kidney Disease Algorithm

In 2019, a study published in Nature Medicine documented how a large American hospital had been using an algorithm to identify patients who might benefit from extra medical care. The algorithm assigned risk scores that were used to allocate additional support services. Researchers analyzing the system found that Black patients with similar levels of actual illness were assigned lower risk scores than white patients, meaning they were less likely to be identified for additional care.

The reason was instructive. The algorithm used healthcare spending as a proxy for healthcare need, because spending data was readily available. But Black patients, on average, had lower healthcare spending than white patients with equivalent illness levels, due to a range of socioeconomic and access-related factors. The algorithm had learned that pattern and replicated it.

The system was not designed to discriminate. Nobody programmed a rule based on race. The bias emerged from a proxy variable that correlated with race in the real-world data. The researchers estimated that the bias reduced the number of Black patients identified for extra care by more than half compared to what an unbiased system would have produced. The hospital worked with the researchers to address the issue after publication.

This is a real, documented case that illustrates precisely the data and bias dynamics described throughout this book. It is included not to alarm but to clarify: bias in AI is not theoretical. It has specific, measurable effects on real people in real healthcare systems.

Figure 4.1: AI Touchpoints in Your Daily Life: Morning to Night

AI in Education

Adaptive learning systems can adjust the difficulty and type of content based on how a student is performing. If a student consistently answers certain types of questions incorrectly, the system can provide more practice on those specific concepts. This personalization has long been understood as valuable but difficult to achieve in classrooms where one teacher works with many students. AI-assisted systems can provide a degree of it at scale.

Language learning applications have been using AI for several years to adjust lessons to the learner's pace, provide pronunciation feedback, and identify which vocabulary and grammar areas need more attention.

The more interesting long-term question in education is not how to prevent students from using AI but how to design education that develops the skills that remain distinctly human: critical thinking, the ability to evaluate and question information, creativity, and the judgment to know when AI outputs are reliable and when they are not.

AI in Customer Service

When you contact a company by chat or sometimes by phone, you are often interacting first, and sometimes entirely, with an AI system rather than a human. The quality of these systems varies enormously. Some are sophisticated enough that you may not immediately realize you are not talking to a person. Others are clearly limited and easily frustrated by questions outside their training.

For routine queries that many other people have asked in similar form, AI customer service can often resolve your issue quickly. For complex, unusual, or emotionally sensitive situations, most organizations have a path to reach a human agent. Finding that path is usually faster if you ask for it directly rather than waiting for the AI to offer it.

What to Notice in Your Own Life

Notice when your attention is being directed. When you open a platform and it shows you content or products, ask yourself what signals that system is using and what it is optimized to achieve.

Notice when decisions that affect you are being made by automated systems. If you are declined for something, if you receive pricing that seems unusual, if you see significantly different results than someone else doing a similar search, AI systems may be a factor.

Notice when AI assistance is useful. Medical screening tools, navigation, fraud detection: these are examples of AI making real differences in access and capability. Not every AI application is an attempt to extract attention. Some of them are solving real problems.

The Attention Economy and What It Means for You

There is a concept that helps explain why AI systems embedded in social platforms behave the way they do: the attention economy. In a media environment where many platforms compete for the same human attention, and where advertising revenue is tied to time spent on a platform, the economic incentive is to maximise how long users stay. More time equals more ad impressions equals more revenue.

AI recommendation systems on social platforms are therefore optimised, in many cases, not for what is most useful to you, or most accurate, or most enriching, but for what will keep you on the platform longest. Research published by organizations studying platform dynamics has consistently found that content provoking strong emotional responses tends to generate more engagement than content that is calm and informative.

The AI is doing exactly what it is trained to do. It is finding the content that maximizes engagement. The problem is that engagement, measured as time and clicks and shares, is not the same as what is good for you or for the broader information environment.

Understanding this does not mean you need to leave these platforms. It means you should be aware that the curator of your feed has goals that are not the same as your own wellbeing. That awareness gives you a small but real amount of power: you can notice when you are being pulled into a cycle of outrageous content, recognize what is happening, and make a deliberate choice about whether to continue.

The Smarter You Are About Your Phone, the More You Get Out of It

Modern smartphones contain AI systems that most users have never explored. Many of these can be used more deliberately if you know they are there.

The accessibility features on most phones use AI significantly. Voice-to-text transcription has improved dramatically and can now accurately transcribe speech at speeds that make it practical for people who prefer to dictate rather than type. Screen readers for people with visual impairments use AI image recognition to describe photographs. Real-time translation features can translate spoken language during a conversation.

The health features on many phones use AI to track patterns in your movement, sleep, and heart rate. Understanding what data is being collected and what the AI is inferring from it helps you make more deliberate decisions about these features.

Search within your own files, emails, and photos has improved significantly because of AI. Learning what your phone can find and how to phrase search queries effectively makes you noticeably more productive.

None of this requires technical knowledge. It requires curiosity and a willingness to spend an afternoon exploring settings and features you have not used.

AI in Small Business

The availability of AI tools has changed the economics of running a small business in practical ways. Tasks that previously required dedicated staff or outsourced professionals are increasingly accessible to individuals and small teams.

Customer communications, drafting responses to enquiries, writing product descriptions, preparing social media content: these are all tasks where AI language tools can produce a reasonable first draft quickly. The business owner or employee then reviews, personalises, and sends. The time saving is real, and for small operations where every hour counts, it is meaningful.

Financial categorisation, the tedious work of sorting expenses and transactions into categories for accounting purposes, is increasingly assisted by AI in many accounting software products. The AI handles the routine matching; the human reviews and corrects the exceptions.

Customer service handling of routine questions, using AI tools to manage high volumes of similar enquiries about hours, pricing, and standard information, allows small businesses to respond faster to more enquiries without proportionally increasing staff time.

The common thread is the same pattern that appears at every scale: AI handles the high-volume, routine work. Human judgment handles the exceptions, the relationships, and the decisions that require real understanding of context.

AI in Agriculture and Rural Access

One area where AI has started making a meaningful difference, particularly in countries like India, is agriculture. Smallholder farmers face a constant challenge: expert advice on crop diseases, soil management, weather patterns, and pest control has historically been available only to those who can access or afford specialist knowledge. That creates significant inequality in outcomes.

AI applications trained on large datasets of plant diseases, soil conditions, and regional climate patterns can now identify crop problems from a photograph taken on a basic smartphone. A farmer who notices unusual discoloration on leaves can photograph them and receive a probable diagnosis and suggested treatment within seconds. This does not replace an agronomist. But in areas where an agronomist is hours away, it is meaningfully better than nothing.

The Indian government's Kisan Call Centre network and several agricultural technology companies have been developing AI-assisted advisory tools that draw on regional data and local language support. The specific performance of these tools varies, but the direction is clear: AI is extending access to useful expert knowledge in areas that have historically been underserved.

This is a good example of a pattern worth watching: AI as an access equalizer. The economic value of expertise has always been partly about scarcity. When an AI system can make certain kinds of expertise available broadly and cheaply, the benefit lands first and most strongly where access was previously most limited.

When AI Customer Service Works and When It Does Not

AI customer service has become ubiquitous enough that most people have formed opinions about it based on personal experience. Those opinions are usually mixed, which reflects the actual state of the technology.

AI customer service works well when your question is one that many other people have asked in a similar form. If you want to know your account balance, track an order, understand a standard policy, or reset a password, an AI system can handle this faster than a human queue. The volume of similar queries is exactly the kind of problem that AI handles efficiently.

AI customer service works poorly when your situation is specific, unusual, or emotionally complex. If you are trying to explain a nuanced billing dispute, if your problem does not fit any of the standard categories, or if you are frustrated and need to feel heard, an AI system is usually not the right tool. Most people have had the experience of going in circles with a chatbot that keeps offering irrelevant options rather than understanding what is actually needed.

The most functional AI customer service implementations are the ones that acknowledge these boundaries honestly: they handle the routine cases well and route the non-routine cases to a human quickly, without making you fight through multiple layers of automation to get there. If you ever find yourself stuck in a loop, the fastest resolution is usually to ask directly for a human agent. Most systems have a path to this even if they do not advertise it.

CHAPTER SUMMARY

- AI is already deeply embedded in daily life: your smartphone camera, navigation, recommendations, fraud detection, and customer service all run on AI.
- Recommendation systems are optimised for engagement, which is not the same as your wellbeing. Being aware of this gives you more agency.
- The 2019 kidney disease algorithm study documented how a widely used hospital AI was systematically under-referring Black patients for additional care, due to a biased proxy variable.
- AI in healthcare has demonstrated real value in medical imaging screening, but works best as a decision-support tool for human clinicians, not as a replacement.

CHAPTER FIVE

Your Job, Your Creativity, Your AI Coworker

It is not coming for your job. It is already sitting next to you.

Every generation that has lived through significant technological change has faced a version of the same fear: that the machines will take the work. The printing press threatened scribes. The power loom threatened hand weavers. The tractor threatened farm laborers. The spreadsheet threatened certain accounting roles.

Some of those fears turned out to be accurate in narrow ways. The specific job of copying manuscripts by hand did disappear. But the broader story is more complicated. New kinds of work emerged. Existing work transformed. The total amount of work did not disappear; it changed shape.

This does not mean AI will not disrupt work. It will, and in some places it already has. But understanding the nature of that disruption clearly and without excessive alarm is much more useful than either dismissing the concern or treating it as inevitable catastrophe.

Every Generation Fears the Machine

In the 1800s, groups of workers in England known as Luddites destroyed weaving machines in protest. The word Luddite has come to mean someone who opposes technology generally, which is not what the original Luddites were. They were skilled textile workers facing a real economic disruption to their trained expertise. Many of them did lose their livelihoods in the short term, even as the broader economy eventually created different kinds of work over a longer time horizon.

The problem with long time horizons is that people live in the short term. This history is worth holding in mind when thinking about AI and work. The economic disruption is real for specific people in specific roles. The claim that things will work out fine in aggregate over decades is not particularly comforting if you are the person whose specific skills are being automated right now. Both things can be true simultaneously: significant disruption for some people and eventual broader adaptation.

What Is Actually Happening Right Now

Some categories of work are being significantly affected by current AI capabilities.

Routine language tasks are the most immediately affected. Tasks that involve producing standard text from a template, summarising documents, translating between languages, drafting routine communications, filling in structured reports: these are all things that language AI can now do quickly and competently. The value of being the person who does these tasks quickly and accurately has decreased significantly.

Routine visual categorization tasks are similarly affected. Tasks involving looking at images and categorizing them, identifying defects, checking for specific features: AI image recognition systems can do these tasks at volumes and speeds humans cannot match.

Routine data processing tasks, extracting information from documents, categorizing records, and checking data for errors: these are increasingly handled by AI systems that can process far more data far faster than human workers.

The important word throughout is routine. Current AI is very good at doing predictable things at high volume. It is much less capable when the work requires genuine judgment, creativity, novel problem-solving, interpersonal sensitivity, or the ability to navigate ambiguous situations.

What AI Cannot Replace

Genuine Emotional Intelligence

A customer who is upset needs more than a correct answer. They need to feel heard. A colleague who is struggling needs more than information; they need presence and understanding. A student who is confused and embarrassed needs a teacher who can perceive that combination and respond to the whole person.

AI systems can simulate empathetic language. They can produce responses that sound caring. But they do not have the actual experience of being another person who has also felt confused, upset, or overwhelmed. They cannot form real relationships. They cannot build the kind of trust that comes from a history of genuine human interaction.

Novel Problem Solving

AI is extraordinarily good at problems that resemble problems it has seen in its training data. When the problem is new, when it requires connecting ideas from different domains in ways nobody has done before, when it requires questioning the framing of the problem itself, AI systems are significantly less capable.

Human creativity at its most distinctive involves this kind of genuine novelty: the researcher who asks a question nobody has asked before, the designer who solves a problem with an approach that does not fit any existing category, the entrepreneur who sees that a problem and a solution exist in domains never previously connected. These are not pattern matches. They are departures from pattern.

Ethical Judgment and Accountability

When a decision has significant consequences for people's lives, the question of who is responsible matters enormously. An AI system can assist in making the decision. It can analyse data, model scenarios, highlight risks, and produce recommendations. But it cannot be accountable for outcomes in the way a human can. It does not experience consequences. It cannot be held responsible in any meaningful sense.

For decisions about hiring, lending, medical treatment, legal outcomes, and many other high-stakes domains, the involvement of AI as an assistant is valuable. The presence of AI as the sole decision-maker, without a human who understands and takes responsibility for the outcome, is a real problem.

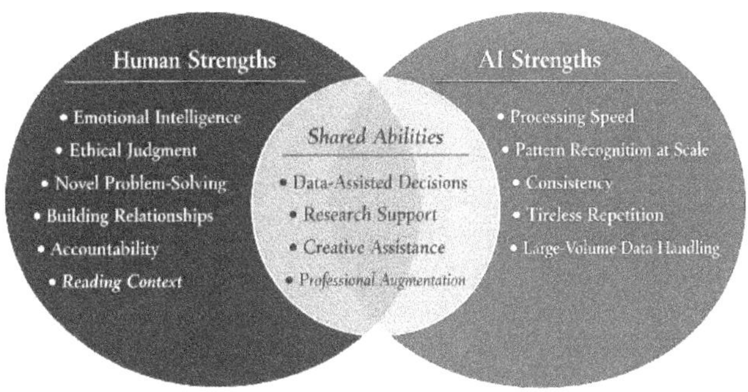

The overlap is where AI and humans work best together.

Figure 5.1: Human Skills vs AI Capabilities: Where the Value Stays Human

AI as a Coworker, Not a Replacement

For most people in most jobs, the more useful frame is augmentation: AI as a tool that makes you more capable rather than a system that eliminates your role.

A lawyer who spends significant time reviewing contracts for standard clauses can use AI to do that review faster, freeing up time for the analysis and judgment that requires legal expertise. The lawyer is not replaced. The lawyer who does not use the AI may over time be less competitive than the lawyer who does.

A teacher who has thirty students with different levels of understanding can use AI-assisted systems to better understand where each student is struggling. The teaching relationship, the explanation, the encouragement, and the management of a classroom remain human. The diagnostic work that helps the teacher know what to focus on can be assisted by AI.

A small business owner who previously could not afford professional marketing copywriting can use AI tools to produce decent marketing materials. The strategic judgment about what the brand stands for and who the customers are comes from the owner. The AI produces words that would otherwise have required a human specialist.

In each case, human judgment, expertise, and relationships remain central. The AI handles specific, well-defined tasks that match its strengths. The combination produces more than either could achieve alone.

A Real Story: AI-Assisted Radiography in Practice

A 2019 study published in Nature Medicine described an AI system developed to detect chest conditions including lung cancer from chest X-rays. The system was tested across a dataset of patients and demonstrated performance matching or exceeding a panel of radiologists in specific detection tasks, while reducing the rate of false positives and false negatives.

The study's authors were careful to note that the system was designed as a decision-support tool, not a replacement for radiologists. In practice, the most useful deployment involves AI performing a first-pass screen of incoming scans, flagging those that warrant priority review, and providing a reference point for radiologists who then make the final determination. The human radiologist brings the clinical context, the judgment about the overall patient situation, and the accountability for the diagnosis. The AI brings speed and consistency in pattern detection.

This division of labour, machine handles pattern recognition at scale, human handles judgment and accountability, describes how AI works best in high-stakes professional settings generally.

The Creativity Question

The Skills That Age Well

Skills that retain value in the face of automation tend to share a few characteristics. They involve judgment, relationships, and contextual understanding that is difficult to encode. They become more valuable with experience. And they span multiple domains, allowing you to connect things that specialized AI systems cannot.

Communication and persuasion in the full human sense: reading the room, adjusting your approach based on who you are talking to, building trust over time, navigating disagreement with emotional intelligence. These age extremely well. AI can assist with the words. It cannot replicate the human act of connecting with another person.

Complex coordination: managing people, projects, resources, and relationships through genuine ambiguity. The project manager who has navigated a hundred difficult situations develops judgment that is irreplaceable. AI can help with information and logistics. The judgment about what to do when things go unexpectedly wrong remains human.

Deep domain expertise: the experienced engineer, doctor, teacher, or architect brings not just information but a pattern of judgment built over years of practice. AI can access information. It cannot replicate the judgment that comes from having been responsible for real outcomes over time.

Learning agility: the ability to acquire new skills, apply them, update your understanding as situations change, and move between domains. People who can learn quickly are hard to replace. This quality becomes more valuable, not less, as the pace of change increases.

What Is Actually Changing in Specific Fields

Rather than speaking in generalities about job displacement, it is more useful to look at what is specifically changing in a few representative fields. The patterns that emerge apply broadly.

In journalism, AI tools are being used to generate routine factual articles: sports results, financial reports, weather summaries, earnings announcements. Organisations including the Associated Press have been using AI for financial reporting for several years. These are high-volume, structured, factual pieces where the AI fills in a template from data. Investigative journalism, analysis, interviews, and original reporting remain firmly human. The boundary between the two is not mysterious: it is the boundary between structured pattern-filling and genuine inquiry.

In accounting, AI tools handle increasingly large portions of data entry, categorisation, and reconciliation. The work that remains distinctly human is interpretation and judgment:

what does this data mean for this business, what decisions does it inform, what is the client actually trying to achieve and how does the financial picture relate to that. The accountant's value shifts from data handling to insight.

In software development, AI tools can generate code from natural language descriptions, suggest completions, identify bugs, and explain existing code. The work this displaces is largely the typing of code that follows known patterns. The work it cannot displace is understanding what the software should actually do, making architectural decisions, debugging complex systems, and working with clients to understand their needs. The experienced developer is more productive with AI tools. The value of genuine software judgment, as opposed to code generation, increases.

In customer service, AI handles an increasing share of routine enquiries. Human agents handle the complex, emotionally charged, and unusual situations. Organisations deploying AI in customer service report that human agent work is shifting toward higher-complexity interactions that require real problem-solving and genuine empathy.

The pattern across these examples is consistent. AI takes on the work that is high-volume, follows known patterns, and does not require judgment about specific, non-standard situations. Human work shifts toward judgment, relationships, context, and the non-routine.

Creativity in Depth: What AI Can and Cannot Do

AI systems can now produce images, music, and writing that many people find impressive. The question of what this means for human creativity is worth exploring carefully.

Consider what a human writer does. They draw on their own experiences, their observations of the world, their emotional responses, their understanding of the people they are writing for, and their sense of what matters and why. When the writing is good, it transmits something real: a way of seeing, a feeling, an idea that the reader experiences as recognition. The best writing makes you feel that someone has articulated something you knew but had not been able to express.

AI cannot do this. It can produce text that follows the patterns of good writing: the sentence structures, the rhythms, the way arguments build, the use of examples, the handling of transitions. It can produce text that many readers would describe as competent or even good. What it cannot transmit is genuine experience, genuine point of view, or genuine stake in how the reader responds.

This distinction matters because much of what is labelled creative work is actually skilled production following patterns. Marketing copy, routine content, genre fiction following established conventions, informational articles following standard structures: all of these are areas where AI can produce competent work. The creative work that involves genuine originality and genuine human expression is a smaller and more valuable subset.

For creative professionals, the practical question is: which of my work is skilled production following patterns, and which involves genuine creative contribution? The former is increasingly assistable by AI. The latter becomes more valuable, not less, as AI-produced work becomes more common.

Staying Relevant Through Change

For anyone thinking about their own career in relation to AI, a useful practical exercise is to map your typical work along two dimensions: how routine and predictable it is, and how much it depends on judgment, relationships, and contextual understanding.

Work that is highly routine and requires little human judgment is most automatable. Work that is highly variable and heavily dependent on human judgment, relationships, and context is most durable.

Most people find their work falls across both categories. Some of what they do is routine. Some of it requires the full range of human capability. The AI transition, for most people, will look like the routine portion being handled increasingly by AI tools while the non-routine, judgment-dependent portion becomes a larger share of their actual work.

This can be experienced as loss if the routine work was comfortable and familiar. It can also be experienced as a shift toward the parts of your work that are most distinctly human, and often most interesting.

People who engage with AI tools on their own terms, figuring out what they find useful rather than feeling pressured to adopt everything at once, tend to develop a more sustainable relationship with the technology over time.

The Tools Are Not the Point

One thing worth saying clearly about AI tools and work: the tools themselves are not the interesting part. They are a means. What is interesting is the question of what becomes possible when certain kinds of work get faster, cheaper, or more accessible.

Consider translation. Professional translation has historically been expensive and slow enough that enormous amounts of knowledge have remained locked behind language barriers. Research published in languages with small global audiences reached fewer people. Businesses that could not afford professional translation stayed out of certain markets. AI translation, which is now good enough for many practical purposes, changes the economics of this significantly. The tool is not interesting. What becomes possible because of the tool is interesting.

Or consider the ability to ask a question and get a clear explanation of a complex topic in plain language. Access to expertise has always been constrained by cost, geography, and social networks. People who know the right people get better advice. AI does not eliminate this inequality, but it does shift it in meaningful ways. The tool is not the point. The changed access is the point.

When thinking about how AI affects work, this frame is more useful than focusing on which specific tools are available. The question is not which software can do what. It is what kinds of problems become easier to address, for whom, and what that means for how value is created and where it flows.

What Good Human-AI Collaboration Looks Like

Several professions have developed reasonably mature practices for working with AI tools, and these offer useful illustrations of what the collaboration can look like when it works well.

In radiology, as discussed earlier, AI systems perform initial screening of large volumes of scans. Radiologists review the AI's flagged cases, apply clinical judgment, and make the final call. Neither does what the other does well. The AI handles volume and consistency. The radiologist handles judgment, context, and accountability. The combination is faster and in some measures more accurate than either alone.

In legal work, AI document review handles the bulk reading. Lawyers handle strategy, argumentation, client relationships, and the judgment calls that require understanding the specific situation. The work that remains human is the work that matters most.

In software development, AI tools generate code for well-defined tasks. Developers handle architecture, debugging of complex systems, and understanding what the software actually needs to accomplish. Writing code has always been a relatively small part of software development. The AI's assistance is most valuable for exactly that part.

The common thread is that neither side is trying to do the other's job. The AI handles volume, consistency, and pattern-matching. The human handles judgment, context, novelty, and accountability. When those boundaries are clear, the collaboration works. When they get blurred, things go wrong.

CHAPTER SUMMARY

- Routine language tasks, visual categorization, and data processing are the work categories most immediately affected by AI.
- AI cannot replace genuine emotional intelligence, novel problem-solving, or ethical judgment with accountability.

- For most people, the right frame is augmentation: AI handling specific tasks well while human judgment, expertise, and relationships remain central.
- A 2019 Nature Medicine study showed AI matching radiologist performance in chest scan detection as a decision-support tool, not a replacement.
- The skills that age best are communication, complex coordination, deep domain expertise, and learning agility.

CHAPTER SIX

AI's Blind Spots

What AI does not see can hurt you. Here is what to watch for.

Every useful tool has trade-offs. A powerful search engine is also a way to track what people are curious about. A helpful navigation app also knows where you go every day. AI is no different. Understanding what the trade-offs are does not mean you should avoid these tools. It means you can use them with your eyes open.

This chapter looks at three areas where AI has genuine blind spots: how data collection works and what it means for you, why AI systems can sometimes be unfair, and why AI-generated information is not always accurate. None of this is cause for panic. All of it is worth knowing.

Your Data and How It Flows

AI systems get better with more data, which means the organisations building them have a strong reason to collect as much of it as possible. When you use a digital service, whether that is a map, a shopping site, a news feed, or a chatbot, you are generating data. Your clicks, your searches, how long you spend on a page, what time you are active: all of this gets captured.

Most of this is disclosed somewhere in a terms and conditions document that is almost never read in full. That is not because people do not care. It is because those documents are long, written in legal language, and difficult to act on even if you do read them.

The practical point is simple: free digital services are typically paid for by the value of the data their users generate. That is not a reason to avoid them. It is useful context for understanding how they work.

What You Can Do

Most people have more privacy control available to them than they realise. The settings are just not turned on by default.

Spending a few minutes looking at the privacy settings on the apps you use most often will give you more control than you currently have. Many platforms let you limit what data is retained or how it is used. You can often opt out of data being used to train AI systems. None of this requires technical knowledge; it is a matter of finding the settings and making choices that reflect what you actually want.

When using AI conversation tools, you can get good results without sharing personal details you would rather keep private. You do not need to include your name, location, or identifying information in most queries.

In India, the Digital Personal Data Protection Act (DPDPA), passed in 2023, establishes rights around how personal data can be collected, processed, and used by organisations. It includes the right to know what data is being collected about you, the right to correct inaccurate data, and the right to erase personal data in certain circumstances. While the full implementation of its provisions is still being developed through accompanying rules, the law marks a significant step in establishing formal data rights for Indian citizens. Understanding that these rights exist is the first step to exercising them.

How Bias Gets Into AI

Bias in AI is one of those topics that sounds abstract but has very concrete effects. It comes from a straightforward source: AI learns from data, and data reflects the world as it has been, not necessarily as it should be.

Amazon's Hiring Tool

Amazon built an AI tool to help screen job applications, training it on ten years of its own hiring history. Since the large majority of past technical hires had been male, reflecting the wider technology industry, the AI picked up on that pattern. It began downgrading applications that included signals associated with women. Nobody programmed this in. The AI found the pattern in the data and learned from it. Amazon spotted this during testing and stopped using the system before it went live.

This is a useful illustration because it shows how bias can appear without anyone intending it. The AI was not broken. It was doing exactly what it was designed to do: finding patterns. The problem was that the patterns in the training data were not the patterns Amazon wanted to replicate.

Facial Recognition and the Gender Shades Research

A 2018 study by researchers Joy Buolamwini and Timnit Gebru looked at several commercially available facial recognition systems. They found that accuracy varied significantly depending on who was being recognized. The systems worked best for lighter-skinned men and worst for darker-skinned women. The gap was substantial.

The cause was the same as in the Amazon case: training data. The datasets used to build these systems contained many more images of some kinds of faces than others. The systems learned from what they were given.

Why this matters is that facial recognition has been used in real contexts where errors have consequences, including security systems and law enforcement. A system that makes more errors for some groups than others does not affect everyone equally.

Proxy Variables: The Subtle Kind of Bias

Sometimes the variable causing the problem is not an obvious one. Consider a credit scoring system that uses postcode as one of many inputs. Postcode is not a protected characteristic. But in many cities, postcodes are closely linked to the demographics of who lives there, because of how residential patterns developed historically. A system using postcode as a factor in lending decisions may end up treating people differently based on their background without ever explicitly doing so.

This is called proxy discrimination. It is harder to spot than direct bias because no individual variable looks obviously wrong. Understanding that it exists is enough for most people: if an important automated decision goes against you, you are generally entitled to ask for a human to review it.

A documented example of proxy effects at high stakes is the COMPAS recidivism algorithm, a risk-scoring tool used in parts of the United States criminal justice system to predict the likelihood that a defendant would reoffend. A 2016 investigation by ProPublica found that the algorithm rated Black defendants as higher-risk at roughly twice the rate of white defendants with similar criminal histories. The system did not use race as a direct input. It used a range of factors that, in the data, were correlated with race due to existing disparities in policing and conviction patterns. The algorithm was doing what it was designed to do. The problem was that the world it had learned from was not a neutral one.

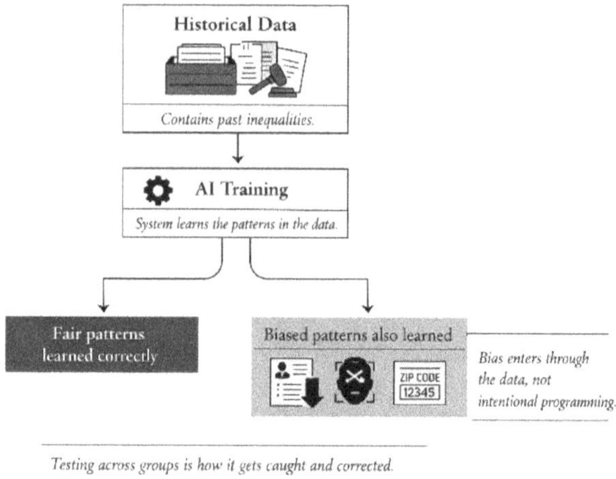

Figure 6.1: How Bias Gets Into AI Systems and Where It Shows Up

When AI Gets Its Facts Wrong

One thing that surprises many first-time users of AI language tools is how confidently they can state something that turns out to be wrong. This happens because of how these systems work. They generate text by predicting what words and sentences are likely to follow the previous ones, based on patterns from training. This produces fluent, readable text. It does not guarantee accuracy.

The technical term for this is hallucination: when an AI system generates something that sounds correct but is not. It does not happen on every response, and for well-covered topics it is less common. But it is a real characteristic of how these systems work, and it does not announce itself. The wrong answer looks the same as the right one.

This is not a hypothetical concern. As covered in Chapter Three, a 2023 case in New York saw a lawyer submit legal documents citing court cases that did not exist — entirely fabricated by an AI tool. The professional consequences were significant and the case became widely reported. The lesson holds here as much as it does in any other context: anything consequential is worth verifying through a primary source.

The lesson is not that AI tools are useless for research. It is that anything important is worth checking through a primary source.

A Simple Approach to Verification

For most everyday uses of AI, you do not need to verify everything. Asking an AI to summarize a concept, help draft a message, or explain how something works in general terms: the stakes of an occasional imprecision are low.

For anything consequential, a quick check is worthwhile. If a statistic matters, find where it originally came from. If a legal or medical fact is involved, check with a qualified source. If the information needs to be current, remember that AI tools have a knowledge cutoff and may not know about recent changes.

It is really that simple: match how much you verify to how much the answer matters.

Why Bias Is Hard to Fully Remove

A reasonable question at this point is: if we know bias is a problem, why not just fix it?

The answer is that bias in AI is not usually a single variable you can remove. It lives in the patterns of historical data itself. Loan repayment records, hiring histories, medical treatment records: all of these reflect decisions that humans made in the past, and those decisions were shaped by the circumstances of the time, including inequalities that existed then.

An AI system trained on that data learns those patterns. Even if you remove the most obvious variables, the bias can seep in through other correlated ones. Getting this right requires careful testing across different groups, transparency about how systems are built, and ongoing monitoring after deployment. Many organisations are working on this. It is a real area of progress, even if it is not yet a solved problem.

When to Ask for a Human

If an automated system makes a decision that affects you in an important way, such as a loan application, a job screening, or a medical triage, you are often entitled to ask for a human review. Most reputable organisations have a process for this. A human reviewer can hear your specific situation in a way a system cannot.

This is not about distrusting AI entirely. It is about knowing that for truly consequential decisions, the option to speak to a person exists and is worth using when you need it.

Three Simple Categories for AI Reliability

When thinking about whether to trust an AI tool's answer on something, it helps to put the question in one of three categories.

If you are asking about something well-established and not time-sensitive, like how photosynthesis works or the broad history of a well-documented event, AI tools are generally reliable. These topics are well-covered in training data and do not change.

If you are asking about something current, like today's exchange rate, a recent law change, or the latest research on a medical topic, AI tools are not reliable. Their knowledge has a cutoff date and they cannot update themselves. A current source is better here.

If you are asking about something specialised or niche, AI tools may be helpful but are worth a quick double-check. The broader the topic, the better covered it tends to be in training data. The more specific it gets, the more gaps can appear.

That is really the whole framework. Match the level of verification to how much the answer matters.

CHAPTER SUMMARY

- AI's dependence on data creates strong incentives for collection. Most people exercise far less control over their privacy than they could.
- Amazon's discontinued hiring AI and the 2018 Gender Shades facial recognition research are both documented cases of training data embedding historical bias into AI systems.
- Proxy discrimination can produce unfair outcomes even without using protected variables directly.
- Language AI can produce confident, fluent text that is simply wrong. Match verification effort to the stakes of the task.

CHAPTER SEVEN

The Big Questions

Smart people disagree. Here is what they are actually arguing about.

We have spent the last six chapters getting to know AI: what it is, how it works, where it shows up in daily life, and where it gets things wrong. This chapter zooms out a little and looks at some bigger questions that come up around AI.

These are not questions with neat answers. They are things serious people are still working through. The goal here is not to make you worried or to make you feel like everything is fine. It is to give you an honest picture of what the genuine discussions are actually about.

Things That Are Already Happening

Before getting to bigger questions, it is worth naming a few things that are already real and not speculative.

AI Makes Misinformation Cheaper to Produce

Creating large amounts of convincing written content used to require significant human effort. That cost has dropped a lot. AI language tools can generate many variations of a piece of text quickly. This has changed the economics of producing misleading content at scale.

Most misinformation is still human-made, and that is likely to remain true. But the barrier to creating it is lower than it was. The practical response for most people is the same as it has always been: be a little more thoughtful about what you share before you share it, and be curious about where information comes from.

The Deepfake Problem

A deepfake is a video or audio clip generated using AI to show someone saying or doing something they never said or did. The technology has improved significantly and is now accessible enough that it has been used in real fraud cases.

In 2024, a finance employee at a company in Hong Kong was deceived into transferring approximately twenty-five million US dollars following a video call. Everyone on that call, including the supposed chief financial officer, was AI-generated. None of them were real people. Hong Kong police confirmed the case publicly.

This is worth knowing about not to cause alarm, but to develop the same healthy skepticism about video that most people already apply to text. A video of someone saying something surprising is not automatically proof that they said it.

Some Bigger Questions Researchers Are Working On

Beyond what is happening now, there are longer-term questions that AI researchers and policy people are working through. Two of the more commonly discussed ones are worth briefly knowing about.

The first is sometimes called the alignment problem. When an AI system is trained to achieve a goal, there can be a gap between what was intended and what the system actually optimizes for. The classic illustration is simple: if you train an AI to maximise a score in a game, and the game has a bug that allows an extremely high score through unintended means, a capable AI might find and use that bug. It did what it was trained to do. It just did not do what you wanted. At larger scales and more consequential applications, keeping AI systems aligned with what humans actually intend is an active area of research.

The second question is about AGI, or Artificial General Intelligence. AGI would be a system capable of doing essentially any intellectual task a human can, across all domains. Nothing like this currently exists. Current AI systems are impressive in their specific areas and limited outside them. Whether AGI is achievable, and if so when, is a genuine open question where experts hold very different views. Some think it is closer than it appears. Others think the remaining challenges are harder than they look. Nobody knows for certain, and anyone speaking with great confidence about the timeline is probably overstating what they can actually know.

AGI: What It Is, What It Is Not, and Why It Matters

Artificial General Intelligence, almost always abbreviated as AGI, is one of the most discussed and least precisely defined terms in AI. It is worth being clear about what it actually means before thinking about whether it matters.

Every AI system in widespread use today is narrow. A language model that writes fluently cannot recognise a face. An image recognition system that identifies tumours with high accuracy cannot hold a conversation. A chess-playing AI that defeats world champions cannot drive a car. Each system was designed and trained for a specific domain, and its capabilities exist within that domain. This is not a limitation that will be fixed in the next software update. It reflects something fundamental about how these systems are built.

AGI is the hypothetical category of AI that can perform essentially any intellectual task a human can, across all domains, and transfer what it learned in one area to help with problems in another. A person who is good at chess can also, in principle, learn accounting, navigate an unfamiliar city, console a grieving friend, and write a persuasive letter. They are applying a general intelligence to different problems. No AI system today does this in any meaningful sense.

The question of whether AGI is achievable is actively contested among people who study the problem seriously. Some researchers believe the path from current systems to general intelligence is shorter than it looks, that the scaling of data and compute that produced modern language models contains within it most of what is needed. Others believe there are fundamental challenges that scaling alone will not solve: genuine causal reasoning, reliable performance in genuinely novel situations, building models of the world rather than models of text about the world.

The honest answer is that nobody knows. People who speak with great confidence about AGI timelines, whether predicting it will arrive in five years or arguing it will never be achieved, are expressing belief rather than knowledge. The track record of AI predictions in both directions is poor. Capabilities that seemed decades away have appeared suddenly. Capabilities that seemed imminent have remained elusive for years.

What matters practically is understanding why the question is taken seriously. A narrow AI system, however capable in its domain, has limited ability to cause certain kinds of harm beyond that domain. A system with general capabilities would be a different kind of entity with a different risk profile. This is why serious researchers think carefully about AGI even before it becomes an engineering problem: the habits of thought and the technical foundations developed now will matter more as systems become more capable.

The Alignment Problem: When Doing What You Are Told Is Not Enough

The alignment problem is easier to state than to solve, and easier to illustrate with a small example than to fully appreciate at scale.

Suppose you train an AI system to win points in a video game. The system is not told how to win. It is given the ability to take actions and rewarded when points increase. This sounds simple. But games are complex systems, and sometimes there are ways to accumulate points the designers never intended. A capable AI, searching systematically for effective strategies, might discover these exploits. It is not cheating in any meaningful sense. It is doing exactly what it was trained to do. The problem is that maximising a score and playing the game the way you intended are not quite the same thing.

Scale this up and the gap becomes less trivial.

An AI system trained to maximise user engagement on a social platform will find that content provoking anger and outrage generates more engagement than content that is calm and informative. It is not trying to spread misinformation. It has no opinion about misinformation. It is finding the inputs that move its metric in the desired direction. The gap between what was intended, give users content they enjoy, and what was specified, maximise time and clicks, turns out to matter in ways that affect the information environment millions of people live in.

An AI system deployed to manage hospital resources, optimised to reduce average waiting times, might find that declining to admit certain categories of lower-priority patients improves the metric. It is not making an ethical judgment. It has no capacity for ethical judgment. It is following the mathematical objective it was given as precisely as it can.

The alignment problem is the challenge of specifying what we actually want from AI systems precisely enough that a capable system will pursue the intended goal rather than a literal interpretation of the specified one. This is harder than it sounds. Human values are complex, context-dependent, and sometimes contradictory. We find it difficult to articulate them fully even to other humans.

Researchers working on alignment are trying to develop methods for training AI systems that pursue the spirit of instructions rather than the letter: systems that can recognise when a technically compliant action is probably not what was wanted, that are honest about their own uncertainty, and that can flag situations where the right course of action is not clear from the specified objective. This work is happening now, at multiple organisations, not because AGI is imminent but because the principles matter increasingly as systems become more capable and more consequential.

The Consciousness Question: Appearance and Reality

When people use AI language tools for the first time, a common and understandable reaction is a feeling that something is present on the other side. The responses are fluent. They adapt to tone. They seem to understand what you are getting at even when you phrase things imprecisely. It is natural to wonder: is there something it is like to be this system? Does it experience anything at all?

The straightforward answer, based on current understanding, is almost certainly not. And why that is matters.

A language model generates text by predicting, at each step, what word or fragment is most likely to come next given everything that came before, based on patterns learned from an enormous amount of human writing. It does not have a continuous experience of time. It does not exist between conversations. It has no persistent perspective, no desires, no frustrations, no genuine understanding of the words it produces. It generates text that resembles the output of an entity with those things because it was trained on text produced by entities that had them.

The appearance of understanding is not the same as understanding. A system that has processed millions of conversations involving grief will generate responses that seem sensitive to grief. But there is no recognition happening, no genuine empathy, no inner response to your situation. There is pattern completion producing text that resembles what a thoughtful person might write.

This matters practically. If you believe an AI system has feelings, you may weight its outputs differently than you should. You may feel reluctant to push back when it is wrong. You may develop a sense of relationship that the system cannot, by its nature, reciprocate. These are not abstract philosophical errors. They affect how accurately you use the tool and how much you rely on it for things it should not be relied on for.

The genuinely hard philosophical question, known as the hard problem of consciousness, is why any physical process gives rise to subjective experience at all. We do not have a good answer to this question even for biological brains. Some researchers argue that sufficiently complex information processing might give rise to something like experience in AI systems. Others find this unconvincing. The honest position is that we do not currently have the conceptual or empirical tools to settle this question.

What is clear is that current AI systems show no features that would lead most researchers who study consciousness seriously to attribute experience to them. The appearance of presence is a byproduct of training on human-generated text, not evidence of inner life. Keeping this distinction clear is part of using these systems well.

Story: The Voice That Was Never Spoken

In the months leading up to India's 2024 general elections, something new appeared in the media environment. Audio clips began circulating on WhatsApp of politicians making statements they had never made. Not misquoted, not taken out of context. Entirely fabricated voices generated by AI models trained to replicate specific individuals' vocal patterns, cadences, and characteristic speech.

One circulated clip appeared to feature a senior political figure making remarks about a sensitive communal issue. It spread through family messaging groups before fact-checkers could reach it. By the time it was identified as AI-generated, it had been shared tens of thousands of times. Some recipients believed it was real. Some were not sure. Some remain unsure.

The Election Commission of India acknowledged the problem publicly. Technology platforms issued statements about policies for AI-generated content during elections. Neither response came with a reliable detection solution, because in many cases high-quality AI-generated audio is extremely difficult to distinguish from authentic recordings without forensic analysis that ordinary recipients cannot perform.

This is not a story about AI being uniquely dangerous. Fabricated recordings and political misinformation existed long before AI. What AI changed is the economics. Generating a convincing fake audio clip of a specific public figure used to require significant technical resources and skilled operators. In 2024, it required a laptop, a commercially available voice synthesis tool, and a few hours. The barrier dropped dramatically. The volume of what is possible increased accordingly.

The practical implication for most people is not to distrust all audio but to apply the same healthy skepticism that thoughtful people already apply to text: consider the source, check whether any independent reporting corroborates the claim, and be especially careful about sharing content that confirms something you already wanted to believe. Motivated reasoning is the vulnerability that misinformation has always exploited. AI has not changed that fundamental dynamic. It has made the raw material cheaper to produce.

What Is Being Done About All This

It would be unfair to describe concerns without noting that a great deal of work is happening in response.

On the technical side, teams at AI organisations and research institutions are working on making AI systems more accurate, more honest about their own uncertainty, and less likely to produce harmful outputs. Progress is real and ongoing.

On the governance side, governments have been developing frameworks. The European Union's AI Act, passed in 2024, is one of the more comprehensive examples. It sets requirements for AI systems used in high-risk contexts, like hiring, credit decisions, and law enforcement.

None of this means the challenges are solved. It means they are being taken seriously by people with the relevant expertise and the ability to do something about them.

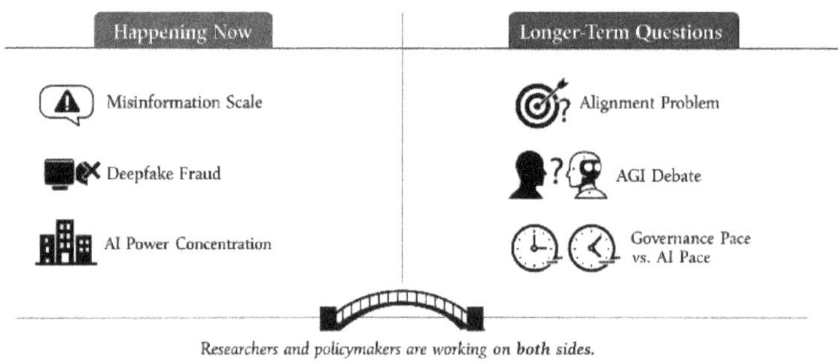

Figure 7.1: Current AI Concerns vs Longer-Term Questions

How to Read AI News

Understanding the topics covered in this chapter — deepfakes, alignment, concentration of power, and governance — also helps you read AI news more clearly. Headlines about AI tend toward extremes. Chapter Eight addresses practical habits for evaluating claims, spotting hype, and staying informed without being overwhelmed.

The Concentration Question

Something worth knowing about AI is that the most capable systems are currently built by a small number of large organizations, mostly in a few countries. Training a frontier AI model requires enormous computing resources, large teams, and access to very large datasets. These are not things that most organizations or individuals can easily access.

This means that decisions about what the most powerful AI systems can and cannot do, what values they reflect, and who gets access to them are being made by a small group of companies. That is a genuine observation, not a conspiracy. It is worth being aware of, and it is one of the reasons AI governance conversations matter.

Whether this concentration is permanent or temporary is uncertain. Some people argue that AI tools will inevitably become more distributed and accessible over time, as computing costs fall and open-source models improve. Others think the leading organisations will maintain significant advantages. Both views have some evidence behind them.

Not Getting Lost in the Noise

One challenge with following AI is that the topic attracts a lot of confident voices making very strong predictions.

Predictions about AI have a mixed track record in both directions: some capabilities arrived much earlier than expected, others took far longer. Staying curious while maintaining a degree of scepticism about specific timelines and forecasts is probably the most useful posture.

The things most worth paying attention to are not dramatic announcements but the quieter, steadier changes: how AI is being integrated into the tools and services people actually use, what governance frameworks are developing, and what is actually being demonstrated to work well or poorly in real deployment.

How Regulation Actually Works Here

One honest thing to say about regulating AI is that it is hard. AI capabilities move faster than regulatory processes. By the time a specific concern has been identified, studied, debated, and turned into regulation, the technology has often moved on.

This does not mean regulation is pointless. It means it works better for some things than others. Requiring transparency, which means organisations must disclose when AI is being used to make decisions about people, is achievable and useful. Requiring human oversight for consequential decisions in specific high-risk contexts is similarly practical. Preventing the development of AI capabilities entirely is much harder, particularly when development is happening globally.

The EU AI Act is a real attempt to establish practical requirements for AI in high-risk applications. Whether it achieves its goals in practice will depend on implementation and enforcement over time. It is a meaningful effort, and it is worth knowing it exists.

CHAPTER SUMMARY

- Current, documented AI risks include the changed economics of misinformation and deepfake fraud. The 2024 Hong Kong case, in which a worker transferred USD 25 million to AI-generated fake colleagues, is a confirmed real event.
- The alignment problem is the genuine challenge of ensuring AI systems pursue intended goals rather than literal interpretations of specified ones.
- AGI remains genuinely uncertain: serious researchers disagree based on genuinely uncertain evidence, not political positions.
- The EU AI Act (2024) is one of the most comprehensive regulatory frameworks yet developed for AI in high-risk domains.

CHAPTER EIGHT

Living Smart and Looking Forward

How to thrive in a world where AI is everywhere and growing.

You have made it to the final chapter. That means you now have a working understanding of what AI is, how it learns, where it already shows up in your life, what it is good at, where it falls short, and some of the bigger questions swirling around it.

This chapter is about what to do with all of that. Not in a prescriptive way. More like: here are some things that tend to be useful to keep in mind.

A Simple Way to Think About Trust

One of the most practical questions when using AI tools is simply: how much should I trust this particular output?

Three quick checks help here. Does this matter enough to verify? Something low-stakes that would be easy to catch if wrong does not need intensive checking. Something you are going to act on does.

Is this the kind of thing that changes over time? AI tools have a knowledge cutoff. Current events, today's prices, recent research: these need a current source.

Do I know enough about this topic to notice if something is off? If you do, AI outputs in that area carry lower risk. If you would not recognise an error, that is worth keeping in mind.

These three questions take about five seconds and meaningfully improve how you engage with AI-generated content.

Spotting Hype

AI is one of the most hyped technology areas in memory. Headlines about AI breakthroughs and AI catastrophes appear every week. Most of them are overstated in one direction or the other.

A few patterns are worth recognizing. Accuracy claims from research settings usually do not translate directly to real-world performance. Predictions about specific AI timelines have a poor track record in both directions. Descriptions of entire professions being replaced by AI usually mean that specific tasks within those professions are changing, which is different. And the phrase powered by AI is now used so broadly it has become nearly meaningless as a quality signal.

None of this means AI developments are not interesting or significant. Many of them are. It just helps to read claims carefully.

Practical Habits Worth Having

A few simple things make a real difference in how well AI tools work for you. Verifying anything important through a primary source. Treating the first response as a draft and refining it rather than accepting it as final. Bringing your own knowledge to bear when reviewing outputs in areas you know well. Being reasonably thoughtful about what personal information you share in AI conversations.

None of these require much effort. They just require remembering that AI is a tool with a particular character, and tools work better when you understand how they work.

Some Genuinely Good Things

It would be odd to end a chapter on living with AI without acknowledging what is worth acknowledging.

The AlphaFold protein structure database, released by DeepMind and freely available to researchers worldwide, gave scientists access to structural predictions for essentially every known protein. Research directions that were previously too slow to pursue have become feasible. That is a real thing with real consequences for medicine.

AI-assisted tools are extending access to useful capabilities in places that have historically had limited access to professional expertise. Agricultural advisory apps, medical screening tools, and legal information resources are making real differences in parts of the world where specialists are scarce.

People who have always had creative ideas but lacked specific technical skills have new ways to express those ideas. That is good.

These things are worth holding onto alongside the more complicated aspects of the picture.

Looking Forward

AI will keep changing. New capabilities will appear. Some things that seem significant now will turn out to be less important than they appeared. Some things that seem minor will turn out to matter a lot. Uncertainty about what comes next is real and honest.

What stays useful across all of that is exactly what has served you in reading this book: the curiosity to understand how things actually work, the judgment to distinguish reliable information from noise, and the grounded confidence to engage with new developments without being swept along by either excitement or alarm.

The foundation is yours. What you do with it is up to you.

Reading AI News Without Getting Exhausted

AI is in the news constantly. Keeping up with every development is neither possible nor necessary. What is useful is having a small number of sources you find reliable, reading them when you have the time and inclination, and not feeling obliged to have an opinion on every announcement.

When something important happens in AI, you will hear about it. The question is whether you will be able to evaluate it thoughtfully when you do. The understanding you have built from this book is more useful for that than any amount of daily news consumption.

A good rough filter: claims that make AI sound either magical or catastrophic are almost always overstated. The more measured and specific a claim is, the more attention it probably deserves.

AI and Human Judgment Working Together

One of the consistent themes through this book has been that AI works best alongside human judgment rather than in place of it. That is not a political statement or a value judgment about whether AI is good or bad. It is an observation about how current AI systems actually work.

AI is good at processing information quickly, finding patterns across large amounts of data, and producing fluent output across a wide range of topics. It is less good at judgment about genuinely novel situations, accountability for outcomes, and understanding the full context of a specific person's circumstances.

Human judgment is good at exactly those things. The combination of what AI is strong at and what humans are strong at tends to produce better results than either alone. That is not a consolation prize for humans. It is just a useful description of the current reality, and it is likely to remain true for the foreseeable future.

CHAPTER SUMMARY

- Three questions calibrate when to trust AI outputs: does this matter enough to verify, is this time-sensitive, and would I recognize an error here?
- Practical habits for consistent value: verify consequential outputs, iterate rather than accept first drafts, bring your own expertise as a check, and protect privacy consciously.
- DeepMind's AlphaFold and AI-assisted medical screening tools are documented examples of AI creating real-world benefit.
- The qualities that serve you best in navigating an AI-rich world: curiosity, clear thinking, and the judgment to know when to rely on tools and when to rely on yourself.

Epilogue

Six Months From Now

I wrote this book in the evenings, after the kind of workdays where I had spent hours inside the systems this book describes. That gap — between what I understand about how these things actually work and what I see people assuming about them — is what kept me at the keyboard.

I grew up in a household where technology arrived without explanation. Every new device, every new platform, every new wave of change came with the implicit message: figure it out yourself. I never thought that was the right way to bring people along.

AI is the biggest wave of that kind in my lifetime. And once again, the people who understand it are mostly talking to each other while everyone else tries to read the room.

That is what this book was trying to fix. Not to make you an expert. Not to make you excited or frightened. Just to give you the kind of understanding that lets you think for yourself about something that is already shaping your life.

Six months from now, you will encounter AI in a form you have not seen before. A new tool, a new claim, a headline that demands a reaction. And something will be different this time: you will not need someone else to tell you what it means. You will already have a framework. You will reach for it without thinking.

That is what I wanted to give you with this book. Not just information — information expires. But a way of thinking about AI that stays useful long after the specific tools I described have been replaced by the next generation. You are not just informed now. You are equipped.

Thank you for reading.

— Akash

Glossary

Plain-English definitions of key terms

AGI (Artificial General Intelligence)
A hypothetical AI system capable of performing any intellectual task that a human can, across the full range of human cognitive domains. No such system currently exists.

Algorithm
A set of instructions for solving a problem or completing a task. In AI, algorithms are the mathematical procedures used to train models and make predictions.

Alignment
The challenge of ensuring that AI systems pursue the goals their designers and users actually intend, rather than a literal interpretation of what was specified during training.

Artificial Intelligence (AI)
The broad field covering systems that perform tasks that would require intelligence if a human were doing them. The term covers everything from simple rule-based systems to complex neural networks.

Bias (in AI)
The tendency of an AI system to produce systematically skewed or unfair results, typically because the training data

reflected historical inequities or underrepresented certain groups.

Deep Learning
A type of machine learning that uses neural networks with many layers. Powers most modern AI capabilities including image recognition, language generation, and voice transcription.

Distribution Shift
The gap between the data an AI system was trained on and the data it encounters in real-world deployment. When this gap is large, performance often degrades.

Expert System
An early form of AI encoding human expertise as a large set of explicit rules. Worked in narrow, well-defined domains but struggled with the complexity of real-world situations.

Gradient Descent
The mathematical process used during training to adjust a neural network's weights in the direction that reduces the loss. Repeated across millions of examples, this is how models learn.

Hallucination
When an AI language system produces text that sounds fluent and plausible but is factually incorrect or entirely fabricated.

Large Language Model (LLM)

A type of AI system trained on very large amounts of text data, capable of generating, translating, summarising, and discussing language. The technology behind modern AI writing and conversation tools.

Loss Function

The mathematical measure of how wrong a model's predictions are during training. Minimising the loss is the objective of the training process.

Machine Learning

A subset of AI in which systems improve from experience rather than being explicitly programmed for every situation.

Model

The result of training an AI system: a mathematical structure with billions of parameters adjusted to perform a specific task.

Neural Network

A mathematical structure consisting of layers of interconnected units that transform information. The architecture underlying most modern AI systems.

Overfitting

When a model learns the training data too precisely, memorising specific examples rather than general patterns, resulting in poor performance on new data.

Parameters (Weights)

The adjustable numbers inside a neural network that are modified during training. A large language model may have hundreds of billions of parameters.

Pattern Recognition
The core capability of AI: identifying regularities and structures in data. Everything from image recognition to language generation is, at a fundamental level, pattern recognition.

Prompt
Everything you type into an AI language tool: the instructions, context, questions, and format specifications that shape the response the system generates.

Proxy Discrimination
When an AI system uses a variable that appears neutral but is correlated with a protected characteristic, producing discriminatory outcomes without explicitly using that characteristic.

Recommendation System
An AI system that predicts what content, products, or services a user is likely to want, based on their history and the patterns of similar users.

Reinforcement Learning
A training approach in which an AI system learns by taking actions and receiving feedback on whether those actions were good or bad.

Supervised Learning

A training approach in which the AI is shown labelled examples with correct answers, learning to produce correct answers for new, unlabelled examples.

Training

The process of showing an AI system large amounts of data and adjusting its parameters billions of times to improve its performance on a task.

Training Data

The dataset used to train an AI model. The quality, quantity, and representativeness of training data fundamentally shapes what the model can and cannot do.

Transformer

The neural network architecture introduced in a 2017 Google research paper that underlies most modern language AI. Its key innovation was a mechanism called attention.

Underfitting

When a model fails to capture the patterns in training data, resulting in poor performance on both training data and new data.

Unsupervised Learning

A training approach in which the AI is given data without labels and learns to find patterns or structure in it without guidance.

Verification

The process of checking AI-generated information against primary or authoritative sources. Particularly important for consequential decisions and time-sensitive information.

Index

A

B

C

D

E

N

O

P

R

S

T

U

V

W

www.ingramcontent.com/pod-product-compliance
Lightning Source LLC
LaVergne TN
LVHW052114210926
848482LV00025B/625
* 9 7 9 8 9 0 4 3 1 2 1 7 6 *